Ten Months
in the
"Orphan Brigade"

Ten Months
in the
"Orphan Brigade"

Conrad Wise Chapman's
Civil War Memoir

Edited by

Ben L. Bassham

The Kent State University Press

Kent, Ohio, & London

© 1999 by The Kent State University Press,

Kent, Ohio 44242

All rights reserved

Library of Congress Catalog Card Number 98-45870

ISBN 0-87338-638-8

Manufactured in the United States of America

06 05 04 03 02 01 00 99   5 4 3 2 1

Frontispiece: Conrad Wise Chapman, ca. 1865.

Courtesy of the Virginia State Library

and Archives, Richmond.

Library of Congress Cataloging-in-Publication Data

Chapman, Conrad Wise, 1842–1910.

Ten months in the "Orphan Brigade" :

Conrad Wise Chapman's Civil War memoir /

edited by Ben L. Bassham.

p.   cm.

Includes bibliographical references and index.

ISBN 0-87338-638-8 (paper : alk. paper) ∞

1. Chapman, Conrad Wise, 1842–1910.

2. Confederate States of America. Army. Kentucky Brigade, First.

3. United States—History—Civil War, 1861–1865—

Personal narratives, Confederate. 4. Kentucky—History—

Civil War, 1861–1865—Personal narratives, Confederate.

5. Soldiers—Confederate States of America—Biography.

6. Painters—Confederate States of America—Biography.

I. Bassham, Ben L. II. Title.

E564.5 1st.c47   1999

973.7'469'092—dc21

[b]   98-45870

British Library Cataloging-in-Publication data

are available.

Contents

Introduction

A T BOWLING GREEN, Kentucky, on September 30, 1861, Conrad Wise Chapman, a nineteen-year-old artist who had come all the way from Italy to enlist, raised his right hand and pledged his services to the Confederate States of America "for three years or the war." Later he wrote: "It was a proud moment to me when I could stand up and . . . swair to serve and never desert the Confederate cause so help me God. I felt every inch a man, and a soldier."[1]

Thus began the extraordinary military career of a highly trained and talented painter who would dedicate his heart and soul to the Confederate cause not just to the end of the war but for the rest of his life. Over the course of the following three and a half years he was to do hard duty in the West, where he suffered a variety of illnesses and survived a serious head wound received at Shiloh; serve for a year in Virginia and see action near Williamsburg; and take part in a significant way in the defense of Charleston, South Carolina. Virtually alone among Civil War artists, North or South, Chapman managed most of the time to combine sketching and painting with his duties as a soldier; and detailed and highly accomplished drawings and oil sketches from his time in three theaters of the war

1. Unless otherwise noted, the lines quoted are taken from Chapman's memoir.

1

have come down to us. Indeed, Chapman's major contribution to the Confederacy was not as a soldier but as the painter who created an artistic record of the Civil War from the Southern perspective. An account of his career and a detailed examination of his art appear in my biography of Chapman, *Conrad Wise Chapman: Artist and Soldier of the Confederacy* (Kent, Ohio: Kent State University Press, 1998).

Born in Washington, D.C., in 1842, Chapman spent his first years in the capital and in New York City. In 1848 his father, John Gadsby Chapman (1808–1889), the then highly regarded artist who painted *The Baptism of Pocahontas* for the U.S. Capitol Rotunda, turned his back on a successful career in America and took his family to Europe. After brief stays in Paris and Florence, the Chapmans settled in Rome in an apartment and studio in the heart of the large Anglo-American art community. There Conrad and his older brother, John Linton, were trained by their father for careers in art. By the end of the 1850s both sons were producing and selling fine pictures of Italian peasants, landscapes, and Rome's most popular tourist attractions. With such a bright beginning, Conrad could have looked forward to a steady and rewarding career for many years as one of the many expatriate painters active in Italy.

But when word of the first battles of the Civil War reached Rome, Conrad, no doubt stirred by the war fever that swept through the small Southern contingent in the city's American community, sold enough work to finance his trip and ran away from Rome to enlist in the Confederate army. After a long and adventurous journey that wound through Paris, London, New York City, Indianapolis, and Louisville, Chapman at last made his way to western Kentucky.

Although Chapman had hoped to fight in Virginia, his parents' home state, he found himself instead in Company D, the "Paducah Company," of the 3d Kentucky Infantry Volunteers, a regiment of the legendary "Orphan Brigade," which had been formed in Tennessee. Gen. Albert Sidney Johnston had ordered the Kentuckians back home to establish a Confederate presence and to protect Southern interests in the state. The army at Bowling Green, numbering some fourteen thousand men, formed the center of the western Confederacy's line of defense. Although Federal troops in Kentucky outnumbered his forces three to one, Johnston kept his opponents on the defensive by cleverly moving his men about to make it appear as if he commanded superior numbers of troops.[2] Chapman and the Paducah Company spent most of the fall of 1861 marching from one camp to the next. "We are a little moving world," he wrote his parents. "Today we are here and tomorrow no one knows where we may be." Some days they would set off on a march and return by train, or vice versa.[3] The deceptions worked so well that, according to Chapman, the people of Bowling Green believed they were being occupied by a hundred-thousand-man force.

Although Chapman's unit saw little real action until the spring of 1862, service in the 3d Kentucky was by no means easy. The artist survived punishing marches, countless nights sleeping on frozen ground, a starvation diet, and at least two devastating epidemic diseases that swept through the camps. But during most of his service in the West he sketched, wrote long and richly detailed letters to his family back in Italy, and kept a journal. William C. Davis has argued that the Orphan Brigade must have been one of the most literate and educated units in the Confederate army. The Kentuckians had their own debating society and glee club, put on amateur theatricals, and assembled a brigade library. Two officers published regimental histories, and two enlisted men, John W. Green and John S. Jackman, wove their wartime notes together with later reminiscences to form two of the most valuable sets of memoirs to emerge from the war.[4] Conrad Wise Chapman, too, brought a measure of sophistication and considerable talent to this cultured band of Kentuckians. He was fluent in Italian, familiar with Latin, knew some French, and had seen a good deal more of the world than his Kentucky companions had. His messmates, amused by Conrad's peculiar accent and a guilelessness he never lost in later years, dubbed him "Rome" and teased him affectionately. A family friend in later years recalled: "Everybody loved Chapman. He was as simple as a child. He gave away or lost almost everything he possessed, and was so innocent and

2. Charles P. Roland, *Albert Sidney Johnston, Soldier of Three Republics* (Austin: Univ. of Texas Press, 1964), 70.

3. Conrad Wise Chapman to John Gadsby Chapman, Camp No. 5, Kentucky, Dec. 31, 1861, Mandeville Special Collections Library, University of California-San Diego.

4. William C. Davis, ed., *Diary of a Confederate Soldier: John S. Jackman of the Orphan Brigade* (Columbia: Univ. of South Carolina Press, ca. 1990), 3.

credulous that he was an amusing study."[5] Delighted at having an artist in their midst, his comrades often exhorted him to draw: "Come, Old Rome, catch it [meaning 'sketch it']."[6]

He began to keep a journal during the autumn of 1861 and made a likeness of each of his messmates next to their names. Unfortunately, this journal, as well as most of the drawings he did during his first months in the army, were lost after he entrusted them to the landlady of a boarding house in Memphis. For reasons unknown, the drawings wound up in a Louisville bookstore, from which they were stolen after the war "by some Yankey soldiers." Writing in 1865, Chapman, who always based his paintings closely on drawings made from life, still felt keenly the loss of those precious drawings, calling them "more valuable than any I could make now, for they are of a more primitive caracter and more strictly picturesh."[7]

He had good reason to miss those sketches, for at the time Chapman was reunited with his family in Rome and was seeking to continue his service to the Confederacy by painting grandiose canvases of its martyred leaders. However, when his principal patron cancelled a major commission and no other buyers stepped forward to order pictures of the war, Chapman was plunged into gloom. One imagines that he wrote the memoir that follows as a form of therapy, so that in the process of reconstructing that lost journal and recapturing on paper the still-fresh memories of soldiering in the armies of the South, he could enjoy those glorious days a bit longer.

He may have planned to publish his memoir, in which case the pages that follow might be thought of as a first draft of a book. The notion is not a farfetched one, for Chapman made it a practice to rehearse his thoughts intended for important letters by writing drafts. And Conrad's father had suggested on more than one occasion that his son publish his Civil War letters.

In 123 densely written pages of a lined and cardboard-bound notebook belonging to his sister, Mary, Conrad set down his reminiscences of the first ten months of that service, from August 1861,

5. John S. Wise to Mrs. Isobelle Bryan, New York, June 7, 1906, Museum of the Confederacy, Richmond.

6. Laura Seager Chapman, "Memoir of Conrad Wise Chapman," Aug. 1920, unpaginated typescript, Chapman Papers, Valentine Museum, Richmond.

7. Conrad Wise Chapman to John Gadsby Chapman, on board the *Louisa Ann Fannie* off Nassau, Mar. 12, 1865, Mandeville Special Collections Library.

when he first heard the news of the "invasion" of his beloved South, to July 1862, when his company joined in the defense of Vicksburg. At the end of the summer of 1862, Chapman requested and was granted a transfer to a unit in Virginia, where he realized his goal of fighting for his parents' native state. By parting company with the Orphan Brigade, Chapman may well have saved his life: of the approximately four thousand soldiers who marched out of Kentucky in early 1862, only about six hundred were left at war's end.[8]

Unlike the account of life in the Orphan Brigade written by Johnny Green, who depended on wartime notes, the memories of fellow soldiers, and newspaper accounts, and that of Johnny Jackman, who made wartime diary entries and other notes he assembled into an edited "journal" near the war's end, Chapman's memoir was written from memory in 1867, aided in part perhaps by references to his extensive correspondence with his family.[9] For the most part very well written in a quite legible, trained hand, Chapman's memoir amounts to a short, entertaining, and informative book that alternately sparkles with humor and bristles with a passionate hatred for the Yankees. Chapman recalls the harshness of life in the field and his dreadful weeks of suffering in a variety of miserable and inadequate Confederate hospitals in a singularly uncomplaining way. Writing from the distant perspective of Italy and out of a growing consciousness of the passing of time that separated him from the comradeship of arms, Conrad remembered his soldiering days, as so many veterans did, with nostalgia, for he suspected those months in the army might have been the high moment of his life. While serving with the Orphan Brigade, he had become "the reckless careless devil of a soldier which do what I ever will in life I shall always be," he wrote. "My character was formed in the armies of the South [and] for better or for worse I must abide by it."

Chapman served as a Rebel soldier, rising to the rank of sergeant, until the war's end. If he continued his memoir past the summer of 1862, those pages have not yet come to light. Indeed, Chapman's papers barely survived at all. Conrad's brother, John Linton, brought many of the artist's letters and the Civil War memoir to America in the late 1870s. When John died, he left his Brooklyn house

8. Davis, *Diary of a Confederate Soldier*, 2.
9. Ibid., 3–4.
10. John S. Wise to Mrs. Isobelle Bryan, June 7, 1906.

and all its contents, according to a family friend, to "a Catholic girl who was kind to him."[10] When this lady, a certain Mrs. Tracey, died in Hollis, New York, in the late 1970s, her daughter sold the contents of the house to a junk dealer. Several years later the dealer contacted Robert B. Mayo, who owned a Richmond art gallery and who at one time had been director of the Valentine Museum. Mayo acquired a group of paintings by Conrad, John Linton, and their father and several boxes of family papers, including some of Conrad's Civil War letters, his 1867 memoir, and John Gadsby Chapman's diary to 1848. A good deal more of the family's correspondence found its way into the Mandeville Department of Special Collections at the University of California at San Diego. Because that library has the lower half of a letter Conrad wrote in Monterrey, Mexico, in 1866, and Mr. Mayo owns the upper half, chances are that the two halves came from the mass of material John Linton willed to Mrs. Tracey. Sadly, according to Mayo, the dealer who bought the estate had consigned to the town dump most of the boxes he found in Mrs. Tracey's basement. Civil War scholars and buffs owe much to Bob Mayo for preserving this important manuscript and for generously giving permission to The Kent State University Press to publish it.

In order to preserve as much as possible of the original character of Chapman's memoir, I have made only slight changes to the text. I did not correct Conrad's misspellings and made only minimal adjustments to his somewhat eccentric mode of punctuation. Chapman often used dashes instead of periods and commas, and I retained his original punctuation except where there might be confusion over when one sentence ends and a new one begins. In addition, Chapman usually placed the name of the month in the upper left corner of each page; here, however, those references to the calendar appear only as changes in the months occur and are bracketed in the text.

Chapman wrote on the left page of his notebook, leaving, for the most part, the right page blank. When he did write a sentence or two on the right side, it is not always clear how he intended those passages to relate to the main narrative. I exercised my best judgment in folding that material into the body of the text.

Finally, a number of individuals, place names, references to Italian dialect, and so forth have been identified, defined, or translated

Photograph of Conrad Wise Chapman taken by his brother,
John Linton Chapman, in 1864. Courtesy of the Valentine
Museum, Richmond.

for the reader. The author is especially indebted to Dr. Giovanna Jackson for her assistance in translating Chapman's occasional uses of the Roman dialect.

The shelves of American libraries already groan under the weight of published Civil War memoirs, so why bring still another one into print? Because Chapman's memoir is such a good "read." His warm memories of camp life before the freezing cold, hunger, and real fighting began, his descriptions of suffering in understaffed, miserable Confederate military hospitals, and his account of his own brief part in the second day of the Battle of Shiloh all make for a powerful and unforgettable picture of the war drawn by a young man with an eye for detail. These reminiscences provide us with a personal account of the war from the perspective of a European-trained artist, an artist who could be called justifiably the South's most important painter of the Civil War era. His memories of service in the West, the first of three theaters of the war in which he served, make one wish that he had continued his manuscript to cover his experiences in Virginia and, especially, in South Carolina, where he carried out the work that has secured him a place of honor in the history of American painting.

Ten Months
in the
"Orphan Brigade"

Rome, September 25, 1867

June 1861

I begin a record to night of my wanderings for the last six years. The dark stormy night that it is, by contrast with the bright summer morning that I first left my home, reminds me of my jubilant hopes for the future then which now are all blasted and my whole life which seems one long stormy night, with here and there a stumble in the dark which may enliven its pages to others but which can never amuse the one who writes them, of himself. However it is a task like another, a pleasure I cannot certainly call it.

My memory holds impressions for a long time, though dates and names fail me. I remember things that happened before I was five years old—Six years is enough to go back—for the present anyhow—

In the month of June, while I was wondering what would be the next news from America, and whether South Carolina's example would be followed by the other states then still in the Union—I was at work, I remember well, in the Studio by my brothers side, we were painting from the same model. A ring at the studio door, the post man is rattling his bajotti[1] and Mary with a paper, rushes into fathers studio. She is back with us in a moment, father sends us the paper, a Paragraph has caught his eye, it is "Abraham Lincolns call for seventy five thousand men to march to Old Virginia and crush the rebellion.[2] Like a flash we both throw our palets aside, animated by the same impulse, and agreed to go into father and tell him what we had determined on—

[*July 1861*] This was to start at once and join the southern army, and when we told father what we had determined, animated by the

1. "Bajotti" is Chapman's misspelling of the term *baiocci*, from the Roman dialect, meaning worthless little coins. (A *baiocco* was an ancient papal coin.) At that time postmen were dependent on tips for much of their income, so rattling the *baiocci* in his pocket was the postman's way of hinting for a tip. The author thanks his friend and Italian instructor Giovanna Jackson for her invaluable help in translating the Italian dialect.

2. The cabinet approved Lincoln's call for 75,000 volunteers on Sunday, April 14, 1861, the same day that Fort Sumter surrendered. E. B. Long, with Barbara Long, *The Civil War Day by Day: An Almanac, 1861–1865* (Garden City, N.Y.: Doubleday, 1971), 59.

same feelings as us, he spoke the words, which in a more guarded moment he never would have—Yes—"Go my sons, and if I was not too old and deaf at that I would go also—" A shadow passed across his brow and I knew at once he would have unsaid those words. It was too late. I knew that in no other way could I have succeeded in getting his consent, and determined to keep quiet and start for the south as soon as I had the means at my disposal to do so. This was not hard to do—, I had a little book of orders, they were not many, but at the lazy rate I had been filling them, they would have lasted me two or three years. I determined to get through them in as many months. I pearched myself by my easel and having an object in view, and a praze worthy one, the first of the kind I had ever had, I worked with a will— On Sundays much against my mothers will and sometimes on the sly, I would be up at my post. What thoughts were mine then, all life and hope, what brilliant dreams now all sunk for ever in the stern riality of the present. Although of a country, which I would thus by helping her in [her] hour of trouble be able to claim as my own— The many friends I would see once more, and remind them of old times in Rome, while fighting side by side with them in the army. Behind it all rose a castle in the air, such as an unexperienced and somewhat romantic mind of nineteen might build. Full of hope for the future[.]

But I soon saw this would be impossible, my father never would have consented to my going, and I feared the power of a Mother and a sisters tears,— This was my last interview with my father on this subject. When he told me to go to work and forget—I saw it would be impossible—My brother was in the country sketching—and his sharp eyes would not be on me. My plans were soon made out—in a week the finishing touches to my pictures would be accomplished, the proceeds six hundred scudi,[3] the largest sum I had ever had, at my disposal. I proposed starting to Paris and had my passport made out, spoke jestingly to my mother and sister of going to the army—, and to several friends here, my preparations were all made by the 19th of August—and as the time approached, I feared that at the last moment, I would give in and show my sadness at leaving home which none but me knew was to be for more than two or three

---

3. Plural of *lo scudo*, a former monetary unit and coin of Italy and Sicily. Before World War II a *scudo* was worth five lire.

months—I knew I could not sit and talk of what I was going to do in Paris—, and have to tell a lie to my father which I had kept from, and determined to sacrifice all rather than do so, I invited some friends and had a supper for them in the little studio which I had occupied. A Yankey in sentiment found his way in our midst, I insulted him perhaps, I did wrong perhaps in my own house—, I became wild with excitement and hardly remember what transpired, the carousal lasted until almost day light. I snached a moments sleep, and my head in cold water I was myself again. My greatest punishment was witnessing the scene of our nights debauching, broken glasses upturned chairs, the atmosphere still reacking with tobacco smoke and the fumes of wine. The Bright clear sun rising in all [*August 1861*] its grandure looked down in reproof on the actors in such a scene, and none could have felt the lesson more severely than I did about to take my leave for perhaps the last time from my family and home. Oh! the sweet sound of that word no one but he who has been for long deprived of one can appreciate—I pass over the parting with my mother and sister and my hurry to the front door, before quitting the house which perhaps I thought then might be for the last time. I stopped to think and take in to its full extent the step I was about to take. I knew what I was leaving, where in the world would I ever meet with those who cared for me one fifth of what they did. Where was I going, what guide had I for the road. I shook off these feelings which would have led me back to where I started, as a duty more sacred than even family ties rose to bid me move forward and meet what ever my fate might be, and prove by my actions that I was a man—In a few hours I was on board a steamer leaving Civitavecchia[4]—, a person was on board whom I knew in Rome, we traveled together, I sought divertion from my trouble and I feared that my feelings might be worked on and after all this victory over them be forced to yield. At Marseilles a few hours and in Paris to dinner the next day—When I took my place at the table, every eye glass in the placed seemed leveled at me, I felt mad with the world in General, and what I had looked forward to with anticipated pleasure I felt a sickening disgust at—Was I in Paris the place I had most longed to visit, and which now I could see no pleasure in. The music from the

4. Civitavecchia, located about forty miles northwest of Rome, was one of the three principal seaports (along with Leghorn and Naples) on the west coast of Italy.

Chateau des Fleurs, the Brilliant many coloured illuminations in the Champs Elizees, the glair and tinsel of that wonderful place, were lost on a forlorn devil like myself. I was alone in a big hotel, I got on top of an omnibus when night came on, and never left it until they stopped running. The Conductor must have been puzzled to know what that silent bird of passage was up to—Some kind friends gave me letters to other southerners bound for Dixie like myself—I took my ticket to New York from Paris finding that the route through Kentucky was the surest to get into the Confederacy—I wrote to Rome telling them what I was about to do—and left the letter in charge of some friends to mail after my departure from Liverpool— How well I recollect the feelings with which I sealed it up and in directing it I tried to disguise my hand, fearing that it might fall in my mothers hands and cause too great a shock. I reached Dieppe from Paris about 5—It was the gay season of the bathing, and flocks of English were packed as thick as herins [herrings] up in Hotel Victoria. At the table d'Haute you could occasional see where a gentlemen sat, but the mass were either from the Cockneys of London or the Epiceries[5] of Paris—and such grabbing it was sick to see. A Yankey sat next to me and in five minutes he told me all his business. In his own estimation no more important man ever walked even the great Roman consuls were nothing compared to him. He was on his mission then to some unknown mud hole of a place in that capacity. He bragged how he was going to pass the Custom house in triumph at New Haven, afford me the same fairly by going under the protection of his spread Eagle[6] advertisement of his office[.] I most respectfully declined, smiled, and watched my man. When we got to New Haven—you could soon tell that you were in old England, by the harsh tone in which the officials answer your questions at the station if indeed they deigned to answer them at all—I showed my baggage amongst the first— a handful of segars cleared me of all trouble, I attempted a cup of coffee, but my then somewhat delicate taste refused the beverage they call by that name—I had forgotten

5. Chapman means *epiciers*, that is, grocers, or, used in a derogatory way, philistines.

6. "Spread eagle," derived from the heraldic emblem popular in the United States, was an American expression associated with exaggeration, extravagance, or effrontery, especially in rhetoric. Albert Barriere, ed., *A Dictionary of Slang, Jargon, and Cant*, vol. 2 (Detroit: Gale Research Co., 1967), 290.

my officious and ostentatious friend, when getting a glimpse in the custom house, as I passed to the train, I saw him there as large as life but not looking as grand as he made out that he would. All his traps[7] scattered to the four winds—, and he with his Bandana to his forehead and his Spread Eagle show bill in his hand, al together a figure for Punch[8]—I sang out, hurry up or you will be too late and there he remained, with a lesson which if he were wise he would profit by to avoid show and bullying especially with English Custom house people. In London I remained but a few hours, sufficient to provide myself with rough substantial clothes and shoes—those shoes how they lasted—I was known by them in my regiment[?] and fellows in camp knew when I had been to the spring for water by their track—Old Rome and his famous shoes, got to be as notorious as Jack and his boots[9]—At Liverpool at the old Grecian Hotel I felt even more alone than in Paris, my little room had not the look of home and the idea of the broad ocean that was to separate me from family and friends—But no—I felt I would find friends and true ones, where I was going. Many perhaps that I had known at home—I little drempt then that many of those I counted on, were quietly away from the news of strife and who probably would have smiled had I told them of my errand. I felt I was going the right way and did not stop to look back—At Dieppe I was half tempted, I do not know how there was an influence about the place—France, I had always liked the French—

At the last moment we were informed at the office of Inman Line that the City of Manchester had been put on in the Place of the City of Baltimore which had been sent to Glasgow for Repairs—and it was where the one we were destined to travel in ought to have been also. She was an old worn out tub her boilers used up and nothing on board worth a rap but her Captain, who was a splendid fellow Capt Halerra—Many of the passengers swore a great deal demanted there tickets back and got off at Queenstown (where the[y] waited for the Cangaroo and beat us six or seven days getting into New

---

7. "Traps," short for "trappings," were one's possessions, especially baggage, personal effects, and other impedimenta. Eric Partridge, *A Dictionary of Slang and Unconventional English* (New York: Macmillan, 1961), 907.

8. *Punch*, the popular British periodical that began publication in 1847, was known for its biting satire and caricatures executed by England's best draftsmen.

9. Perhaps Chapman is confusing "Jack and his boots" with an anecdote about George "Harden" (G. O. Heyden) and *his* boots related later in the narrative.

York[10]—We had a voyage of 19 days—and what long ones they seemed to me. Capt Petit from New Orleans a regular fine old specimen of a sea captain, Capdeveille[11] from the same place who had been studying medicine in Paris, and was sighing over the loss of his Mistress, were the two I had letters to, and they and the Capt. were the only ones who knew my plans. Trust and Shipley I never heard what became of them in the war. Others on board, rash fellows from the south, made it too warm for the Yankees on board and got up a club and named it Bull Run,[12] of course I fell in with the rest, but kept quiet in the corner while I let them do the talking and proposing the healths of our different leaders—, for I did not know who to trust. I was right for once for we afterwards found that a Yankey spie had got in our midst— We smoked gossipped the time away, until segars gave out and hard tack made its appearance at dinner, and no land in sight— The game of shuffel boards lost its interest, but as we had plenty of provision, such as it was on board, we felt in no allarm. The sailors got up some fun for us and the steerage was crowded with the cabin passengers. The sailors and the Irish Biddis[13] were cutting up great shines—I went over with a lovely veiled figure and was soon as gay as the rest. On our side we had occasional social [illegible]—but the other side of the house was not invited of course, and this brew[ed] amongst the three hundred in the stearage a mutinous feeling, and some swore they would pass the rope that marked their line, and some were bold enough to step across in defiance of the Capt—The ringleaders were soon in irons—and quiet again reigned on board. The Capt on this accasion showed the man he was by stepping in the midst of them and the mates followed, it was night and the ladies on our sides were preparing to faint when it ended—No other event marked our life on the City of Manchester except D.C. who had found out our would be friend as an impostor

10. The *City of Baltimore* was scheduled to sail from Liverpool on August 28 and the *Kangaroo* was set to sail from the same port on September 4. The *City of Manchester* arrived in New York on September 16, 1861. *New York Herald*, Aug. 25 and Sept. 17, 1861.

11. Auguste Capdeville. See note 94.

12. The Battle of Bull Run, or First Manassas, an overwhelming Southern victory, was fought July 16–22, 1861. Long, *The Civil War Day by Day*, 95–100.

13. In the nineteenth century, "biddis" were young women. Partridge, *Dictionary of Slang*, 50.

and spie and waited for him on deck by moonlight and dressed him up in style—He however took it like a Dog with the insults heaped on him on all sides, and kept his revenge warm until he could get us on shore where he turned us over to the mirmidons[14] of the Law, as Southerners who were bound for the Southern army, and at the custom house they showed us no quarter, they fell on me as a nephew of Genl Wise,[15] and after ransacking all my trunk hunting for a false bottom to it, took me in a private room for personal examination— they looked in my pockets or at least made me turn out what I had, I slipped a paper from one hand to the other, they looked wise, oh so wise[.] I kept my countinance and at last gave up to them the coveted paper which I knew the fools could not read, it being the written direction they gave me in Paris when I took my ticket for New York— That is what we want, they thought they had found a mares nest— An Interpretor was soon found and they looked quite cressfallen at the failure, and let me off after examining the lining of my hat—and refusing to look into my boots which told them I was ready for them to pull off. All the rest of the party, Eleven of us, had gone through the same inspection—and we thought we were clear to go to the Hotel, and enjoy the glorious liberty of being in the land of the free—but no such thing[. A]t the door we met a party of Policemen who took us in charge, and our baggage was packed on one dray, and we in the other with a couple of Policemen one inside and one up with the driver—and a crowd of little boys following us calling out there go the secesh, in this style we rode up Broadway—I asked the Policeman to please let me know when we got to Great Broadway, and when he told me I laughed out right, and remarked to the rest that the bye streets in Paris were wider—And you call this Broadway sure enough. What a place—at the Police station we were informed we could not leave until we underwent another inspection

14. "Mirmidons," from the Italian *il mirmidone*, are a constable's attendants or assistants. The term is derived from a story in Greek mythology in which Zeus changed ants into human escorts, called Myrmidons, for Peleus on his visit to Phthia; hence, it is a derogatory name for minor police officials.

15. Brig. Gen. Henry A. Wise (1806–1876), a former congressman from Virginia, secretary of war, and state governor, was a good friend of Chapman's father. Conrad received his middle name to honor Wise, and this may have led New York City authorities to assume the artist and the general were related.

and had been questioned by the Chief of Police Kennedy[16]—One of our Party knew the man, he went in and had a chat with him, and he returned our confiscated wickers and other property or rather the order for to get them and turned us loose. When we got out we of course were at a loss how our friend Capt from Maryland got us off. Do you know what we were taken up for, it was for drinking the Health of Jeff Davis, and I turned it off as a joke by saying we did not neglect the Health of John Brown so we ought to be quits—We hastened to the Hotel and coming down to dinner the evening paper was handed to us with an article headed in Big letter descent on seacssionist in which we all figured and perhaps were photographed while we were at the Police station besides. I looked at my name in print, and had to confess I never had drempt of its coming into notoriety that way—The next morning the Herald I believe made a wonderful story out of it. Capt. Hallera was on shore and we had a night of it commencing at the Oyster Saloon close by and ending in the Maison Doree—We went to the the Circus where the clown showed us how Jeff Davis would look at the end of the war and various other entertaining subjects in the same line—Every step we took we had the eye of the Police on us, we amused ourselves by going from place to place and their eyes never left us. Talking at the Fifth Avenue Hotel we had to take the causion of watching the doors, to guard against eves droppers. Our Consil of war decided it would be improvident for the four or five of our party that were together to travel thus and that it would be more prudent to brake up and meet some where. The Rendezvous was given at Louisville at the Galt House,[17] and we each took separate times to start—and I was the last that was to leave. The Capt.—was first—Mr. H. from N.C. second and the Dr. next. As the Dr. was about to start he took me aside, and begged me to turn back while there was yet time and not

16. John A. Kennedy served as general superintendant of the New York City police from 1860 to 1870. Said to have "ruled with a hand of iron," he was attacked and severely beaten by a mob during the draft riots in the city in July 1863. James F. Richardson, *The New York Police: Colonial Times to 1901* (New York: Oxford Univ. Press, 1970), 119, 136.

17. The Galt House, built at the corner of Main and Second Streets in the 1830s, was one of the two leading Louisville hotels. "The cream of Southern society summered here," and Charles Dickens, among other notables, stayed there on his visit to Louisville. Isabel McLennan McMeekin, *Louisville: The Gateway City* (New York: Julian Messner, 1946), 106.

sacrifice myself. It was too much, I asked him if he was a Southern man at heart, and why he tried to persuade me to do what he would not do. Turn back yourself but I go on—After the Dr. the last of our party left—I went around to fathers old friends the Kembles.[18] I found them all out of town except Gove and he had gone out—I maid up my mind to see him, and so I went in and found his cousin or some Yankey relation there, to whom I made myself known, he at once remembered my father and all about me. He proposed to surprise Gove on his return and introduced me as Mr. Valentine.[19] We vowed we had neither of us seen each other for fifteen Years—he did not recognize me. I made myself perfectly at ease, and he looked at me in astonishment, at last I ended the farce by making myself known, and went into their little gallery to see my fathers pictures, and I told him which way I was bound for and my purpose in going to the south—He was astonished and wished to give me letters to Genl Scott[20] so that I might go by the way of Washington to Virginia. I thanked him, but told him I had my road clear enough without the help of as great a man as Genl Scott. That night I was already to start the next morning, and while he was waiting for me to go up to Cold Spring,[21] I was rattling away on the cars westward—No incedent happened on the road until I reached Indianapolis where we were obliged to lay over the best portion of the day as the train which was ahead of us had run off the track—While waiting in this Hateful hole of a place and wondering about in disgust at the whole

18. Gouverneur Kemble was the youngest son of William Kemble, John Gadsby Chapman's good friend and business agent. Edward De Lancey, *Collections of the New-York Historical Society* (New York: New-York Historical Society, 1885), xxi.

19. Chapman is probably referring to Edward Virginius Valentine (1838–1930), another artist—a sculptor—from Virginia who was in Europe to study art and to take the Grand Tour between 1859 and 1865. In fact, Valentine called on Chapman's family in Rome in 1861. Valentine's best-known work is the marble figure of Robert E. Lee in the chapel at Washington and Lee University in Lexington. Charles Reagan Wilson and William Ferris, *Encyclopedia of Southern Culture* (Chapel Hill: Univ. of North Carolina Press, 1989), 129.

20. General in Chief Winfield Scott (1786–1866), a Virginian, was head of the Union armed forces until he was replaced by McClellan in November 1861. Mark M. Boatner III, *The Civil War Dictionary* (New York: David McKay Co., 1959), 728–29.

21. Cold-Spring-on-the-Hudson, situated on the east bank of the river opposite West Point, was the location of the Kemble family seat and the cannon foundry (chartered in 1818) that made the family's fortune and reputation. De Lancey, *Collections of the New-York Historical Society*, xx.

Yanky race and their way of living, we returned to our Hotel, if a smoky dingy tobacco sprinkled whisky shop could be designated as such, the most of the inmates of which were on a par with the establishment. They were mostly loafers who seemed to have nothing to do but whittle away the benches and chairs which were many of them nearly used up in this way—and squirt tobacco juice—One of the trains that came in brought a prisoner, the crowd gathered at once. I was not long before I learned it was a southerner Governor Moorhead[22] who had been arrested in Louisville. I wondered why the fellows who were so fearce against the rebels and enjoyed the sight of an old man being taken away from home, did not try and get something else to whittle than the inofensive benches in a tab [tap?] room—The military were beginning to stir about, they were then dressed in gray, but they now changed it to blue. . . . These fine broadcloth soldiers were quite pretty to behold, and their fair Yankey galls were feasting them with Pumkin pie and I don't know what all— I felt very sad the only southerner perhaps except myself in the very hotel with me a prisoner. It was time to start, and when we did get off how we went? When a short distance from Indianapolis we fell in the train which had most innocently taken to the fields instead of the railway tracks, we found that no one was hurt and all ready to go on to Louisville with us. I got into the sleeping car for the night, had a birth fixed up and was just about turning in, when some one caught hold of me by the leg from the birth below. I was quite taken aback for I had been uneasy for some time thinking I was watched by some suspicious looking chaps I caught several times with their eyes on me—When I got over my shock of nerves and looked down, what was my surprise to find that the arm I had grasped belonged to no other than my fat fellow traveller the Capt. who had started before me. He whispered in broken English, when you see one me in the morning, don't recognize, we are watched, watched

22. "Gov. Moorhead" was Charles S. Morehead (1802–1868), governor of Kentucky from 1855 to 1859. He worked hard to avert Civil War and to maintain his state's neutrality. When he opposed furnishing troops to the national government, he was arrested on September 18, 1861, on suspicion of favoring the secession of Kentucky and was kept in Federal prisons until paroled in May of the next year, whereupon he fled to Canada and then lived in Europe and Mexico before returning to the United States after the war. *The National Cyclopedia of American Biography*, vol. 13 (New York: James T. White, 1906), 8.

by G——. The Capt. had been passing himself off as a French man that could not speak English and swore he would report to the French Consul at Louisville if they touched one of the trunks and so got through scot free. When we reached Louisville we found the Dr. and our North Carolina friend, who was by the by an Englishman by birth, and a third person who saluted us with the southern pass word here's your mule.[23] His story will show up how the right men were flocking to the south. His name was Hull [Hall?], he was born in Alabama, and was in [*September*] business in New York, he was a youngster like myself—and made up his mind [to] brake off with his employers and start and the only way he could do so, as those they were relatives of his family was to give them the slip, so one bright morning he got them to send him west on business for the house and he did not stop until he reached Louisville and proposed going on with us. Capdeveille had been attracted to his bold outspoken sentiments against the south and his making friends with a Yankey officer in the car—so bitter did he get at one time that the Dr could hardly contain himself, but when they got aside they both got to be good friends—and it seemed that he was known by this U.S. Officer and it was his only resource to put him off his guard for it looked suspicious his going so far from his business beet. We were now five conspirators, and amongst the five, but for the English N.C. we would have been balked just as we began to see land in sight. as no one could leave Louisville without taking the hateful oath of elegiance. Many took it and say openly they did not regard it anymore than

23. "Here's your mule," a nonsensical expression of immense popularity in the Rebel armies, has mysterious origins and even more mysterious meaning, if any. Bell Irvin Wiley quotes this account from a veteran's diary: "The first I heard of it was this—some man in the neighborhood had lost an old gray mule and was . . . enquiring for it among the regiments—Co. B had straw in their tents to sleep on. . . . . . Among them Tom Nance . . . his hair was very thin on his head and his ears seemed all the larger for it—Under the general excitement of the day he laid down in his tent to sleep—some lively fellows roving about . . . happened to look in Tom's tent and being struck with his appearance called out for the mule man—Here's your mule others came to see and repeated the saying . . . and fun and yeling being the order of the day the words soon reechoed alover the camp and those adjoining and became a by word everywhere." Wiley, *The Life of Johnny Reb: The Common Soldier of the Confederacy* (Baton Rouge: Louisiana State Univ. Press, 1988), 382n. "Here's Your Mule" was a Confederate camp song with a similar theme. W. L. Fagan, ed., *Southern War Songs* (New York, 1890), 319–20.

worthless paper. Had I have taken it, which I would not have done to save me even from prison, I would have [never] considered it binding for an oath can never be forced. Each one had his pet scheme for getting out of the Yankey clutches but an other day had passed. Louisville each day was getting harder to get out of, troops were going[?] in, cheered by some and pelted by others. What was to be done. The Englishman decided it[. H]e got five special permits for us, and a custom house officer inspected our traps. I had nothing he could make capital out of, and so I let him alone as he tossed my traps about looking as savage as a meet axx with his revolver peeping from under his coat. I only found out afterwards what the cur was pouting about, when his tone immediately changed as he opened Petits trunks one by one and gently shut them again, in each of which Petit, that old roge, dropped a gold piece which the other one pocketed. When we got south he told me if that fellow had dived in those trunks it would have all been lost. At last we were on board the steamboat for Henderson. Our trunks safely put away with the mark of special permit on them. An American Steamboat, this was the first I had ever been on since infancy, what an outlandish thing it is, how quiet you move on like a dream, and certainly if I was inclined that way, it was just the afternoon for a day dream, seated near the balustrade many southern ladies on board I breathed a new atmosphere from what I had felt in American before. On both sides of the river waved flags of the two different, and how different, sections of country, the Confederate and the flag which had had it origin in blood shed of independence and which was to be disgraced by those who had but little share in giving it birth. How soon was I to see that same flag desecrated by the race who now claimed the right of fighting under its fold. Many were the thoughts during the quiet of that glide down the Tennessee to Henderson, which we reached that night. We landed put up at the Hotel, some pretty ladies were staying at[.] I was cautious at first for I did not know my ground. But when the notables of the Place called on us, and amongst them and old family friend of fathers, and they told us we were on free ground. At last I could give vent to my pent up feelings and the hall rang with our hearty Cheers for Jeff Davis and the Confederacy, drinks were brought of all kind, and plenty of pine to whittle, some how or other the fellows choowed as much as at Indinapolis and the chairs held the same mark of ilusage on them, but I rather admired the operation and indulged in a whittle myself. It was no longer Yankey for me. The town that night was in one great commotion till morning, such shouts and to do, the next morning at breakfast excused us a[s] soldiers. . . . Some thought the fat Captain would have to loose some of his flesh before undertaking a double quick. We got a wagon at last at an enormous expense I forget how much and four mules for Columbus Ten, as we had to go through the bush whackers of Hopkinsville, and run the risk of jayhawkers and Union scoundrels[.] A party had gone on ahead and we might possibly overtake them. Next morning we were to start. Our grand imposing conveyance stood at the door, I wrote a hasty note to Rome saying I was in Dixie all right at last. The Capt. perched on one of the trunks, the softest seat he could get, with an enormous umbrella over his head to keep of[f] the sun, but which we soon made him close. as the young ladies made their appearance to give us a farewell and his shade was in the way. We all stood up and gave them the hearty cheers and all the by standers joined in when the lusty ones more came for Jeff Davis and the Confederacy, even the driver chimed in, and with "Here's your mule and a crack of the w[h]ip," we started the ladies God bless them still waving their handkerchiefs as we went out of sight, which the Capt was the only one who did not seem to appreciate fully, on account of the jostly wagon and his hard seat—

The first place we stopped at after leaving Henderson was at a little Kentucky homestead by the roadside. A pretty little woman bid us welcome at the door and returned our salute as we drove up of "here's your mule." You are going the right way my friends, and you shall have the best in the house, my husband has gone to the wars, and I have given up accomading passengers on the road—and such a dinner that she gave us, we got merry on the old man's cider, and with our pipes in full blaze started again on the road to drive. As night came on, precautions had to be taken against the Union scoundrels of Hopkinsville and other independent jay hawkers—so Hall and Eye formed the advanced guard, and were working along in a most unconcerned way possible, thinking the stories we had heard at Henderson nothing but hoaxes. When we were brought to a halt, "which way, and on what business" was the demand of the boorish sentinel. Oh! "we are good Union," answered Hall. "I did not know you stopped people going to Hopkinsville, we belong to the party ahead and others are following[." W]e did not go on until the others got up and we could agree on what to do should we be attacked.

The next day we got up with the other party soon after leaving Hopkinsville, the Union den, in the distance and our driver cracked his whip and cursed the mules and was more jolly than ever. [*Facing page:* The other party was our fat official of the boat who said he did not regard Yankey oaths, and his wife and an Indiana deserter which they had picked up on the road and were taking him to the southern camp as he said he had mearly deserted to get south.] "Now from here on you have nothing to apprehend[,] all are friend[s].["] And he "here'd your mule" at every house we passed. At twelve oclock we stopped at Mr. Christian B. Garrets place for dinner. A camp of volunteers was just outside of his fence. They were Confederates who I supposed at the time were in earnest, and so decided to join them at once— We dined with old garret his wife and seven daughters, from 6 years old to 20— The old lady was evedently a tartar, I owe her a grudge for after finding out I intended joining the boys outside, in their volunteer corps, said it looked funny, but satisfied her self with warning me of the fate which befell spies in the old revolution. Their overseer was in this same company, and no doubt kept an eye on me all the time. In spite of this little disagreeable incident I desided to remain and join them for several reasons— One was that my little supply of funds was on a rapid decline and was in the last stages, secondly if I had come over to join the army I might as well fall in where I was, I had not the means of getting to Virginia without the proferred help of my traveling companions, and I knew certainly no one here, but further on I would be no better. I felt sorry to part with my four friends, but my trunk was tumbled over to me and I bid them good bye and all wished me good luck I know. So there I stood by a roadside in Ky—, if not regularly a soldier at least not far from it.

Old Christian B. Garret was a ritch character, no writer ever found a better hero for a story[. H]ow much I regret that I have not the pour to do his and his old castle of a place justice—, for the first night as there was no guard to mount I slept in the overseers house. And the old fellow came in to keep us company and took me down to his blacksmith, who was filling the part of vulcan when we went into his place that night, and with his negroes was turning out huge knives by the dozens. Old Garret was having them made for his friends, and told me with a wink he could use one himself when wanted. I took a great fancy to him, and he did to me in spite of the old ladies evil forbodings about my fate— The most of the night I entertain[ed] the old chap, with wonders of Rome[.] The old fellow was a sharp one and knew much more about the sights to be seen there than I, and so I did not attempt any of my yarns, which afterwards made me so popular in the ranks. Almost his last words to me when I was about to leave him were— You are in earnest go and fight the battles of the south and if you are ever in difficulty call on me—

The next day I reported to the camp the headquarters of which were at the blacksmiths. Each man I met there wanted me in his company. The aquisition of two or three members often turned the elections of the officers and I suppose they wanted all the green ones they could get—, and I must have appeared to them of that stripe as much as my Yankey Companion the deserte[r], who had turned back on the road to join me. I was not very proud of my company of course, but after all he was a good enough sort of fellow as much so as any Yankey ever gets to be, and ready to serve the south which made him one of us for the time.— At last several Captains who had just been elected made their appearance, one old fellow seemed of the right stamp and I decided to go in with him and his boys, he was to get me a horse and equipments,—My Indiana friend joined also, I remained all day with the party, drilling but soon saw they were all in for a frolick, more than soldiering in earnest. I thought if all the southern armies, were like this little one it must be very much like a farce. I felt foolish after my long journey from Rome, to be thus placed with a bad unorganized troops bent more on their frolicks and dances with the girls in the neighborhood than towing the mark as Confederate soldiers. [*Facing page:* Their camp fires and splendid set suppers of all the delicacies of the seasons were not of the genuine stamp too many negroes to wait on them and too many good things. I enjoyed the novelty of the scene, which certainly looked as Romantic and picturesk as the eye could wish for but then it lacked the reality which I was after. I asked myself was I a confederate soldier, and the whole thing looked doubtful. Six months was the time they talked of going in for. Did all go in for that time or was they no regular army in this country, I asked myself.]

I told the Capt as much, and he agreed with me and as I had not

been sworn into his company he had no hold on me any way. That
night we bivouacked in the Blacksmith's shebang[24]—and in the middle of the night as is generally the case with troops first out in the
field an alarm took place, great comotion on all sides, but quiet once
more was restored and a few hours of refreshing sleep prepared
both me and my companions for our walk to Clarksville on our route
to the Army in Bowlingreen.

We bid all our recent comrades goodbye the old blacksmith in-
cluded with the promise to welcome them in the army when they
came there. We next went to the Garrets house, where I left my
trunk (one of the many I have lost) taking a change of clothes in a
small bundle which at the end of a stick I swung on my back. My
partner did the same with his, and thus we started on our pedestrian
trip— As we walked along side by side I could not help but think
over the queer changes I had gone through in one short month.
From Rome to find myself walking on through a strange country
with one little gold piece left in the world and an still more uncer-
tain fate until I reached the Army. Mrs. James famous two military
horsemen[25] came to my mind and we both wished before night we
had been as lucky. What little I had in the way of money I wanted to
save for an emergency to get from Clarksville to Bowlingreen, so
we had to make our dinner off of the Apple trees along the road[.]
[W]hen we got to the state line and we were realy in Dixie, my
partner treated to a drink of cider and some ginger cake and with
this and some tobacco in our pipes we went jogging on at a much
better rate.

When we reached Clarksville, the steamboat was about starting
for Nashville, I thouht of our old friends the Yeatmans there and
how glad they would be to see me. I had just enough to pay my
fare—but what would become of my friend. By going to Nashville I
moved off my track and so I determined to stand my ground. The
next thing was to find a quiet place for the night where my little
stock of money would be able to stand the bill. I looked at the Grand
Hotel of the place and it was rather hard to turn into an inn like
sailors have in Seaports instead. It was false dignity and I crushed

24. Today it means "the whole thing," but in the nineteenth century it was slang
for a hut, shop, or dwelling. Partridge, *Dictionary of Slang*, 752.

25. This is probably a reference to the writings of Mrs. Edwin James, author of
Wanderings of a Beauty: A Tale of the Real and the Ideal (New York: Carleton, 1863).

it at once. We were well received by our host and hostess, and a sparkling fire was made in the parlour kitchen where we spent most of the night, so all together I was better off than in the Grand Hotel after all. An English enjenier on the railroad and ourselves were the only boarders. He was musical and with songs and ritch stories the night passed pleasantly by. I had not got over what ever since I left Rome had followed me, that was excessive politeness to persons especially women speaking English, and where in Italy I would have felt myself perfectly at ease in an Osteria,[26] here caught myself talking as if in our parlour in Rome. Much to the Englishman and Yankey friends amusements. Even on the road I touched my hat as I would to some old Padre or pretty contadina[27] in Italy and if I looked back I could see the stairs that followed me as if I was a newly imported wonder. But to return to our Hd quarters at Clarksville.

The Engenier proved a usefull friend—he put us on the track of how to get to Bowlingreen— [I]f we failed in other way he offered to take us in himself. In the mean while I went up to the station to see if I could find anyone who would pay our fare on for the use of us as soldiers. I soon succeeded in finding one who wanted two good reliable dare devil chaps he said they must be, to join his independent troupe of Guerillas. I told him I was his man, and agreed to meet him next night if my partner liked the idea. I had a long talk with Indiana, I will call him so as his name I cannot recall at present and he said if we could not do better we would always have time to decide. Next morning our host said that I might learn a great deal that I wanted to know from Col. Tylgman[28] of the 3rd Kentucky who was in town. So I polished myself up as best I could and called on him. I found him beautifully fixed and enjoying the lovely morning that it was in a loose dressing gown on his piazza surrounded by flowers. I made known my purpose at once, and he advised me to join the Paducah Company of which he had been Capt—, and said I

---

26. An *osteria* is an inn, a tavern, or a public house.

27. A *contadina* is a young country girl; a peasant girl.

28. Col. (later Brig. Gen.) Lloyd Tilghman (1816–1863) organized the 3d Kentucky Regiment at Camp Boone in July 1861. He was made inspector and commander of Forts Henry and Donelson. He was captured when Fort Henry was taken by Grant in early February 1862. After being exchanged, he led forces at Corinth and at Vicksburg before his death in May 1863 at Champion's Hill. Boatner, *Civil War Dictionary*, 840.

would find them a jolly set of gentleman and good well diciplined soldeirs—He gave me a free pass by rail to Bowlingreen for myself and Indiana and told me I could start when I wanted. I walked in to our Domicille showed my papers, and told Indiana the army was at Bowlingreen if he wanted to go, if not I should go alone for of late I began to think he was going to back out. Though poor fellow he fought it out to the last and was killed in the Artillery Com—he enlisted into.[29] We packed up and our host after much persuasion agreed to accept half what he charged other folk, the hostess put us up something for the road and I think gave a sly wink to Indiana, but I might have been mistaken. Our English friend got steam up and with a ginger bread to munch and some segars to smoke we were all spry for the trip to Bowlingreen, and I had still out of my little fortune a few dimes. At the station I got a glimpse of our Guerilla man, and he looked daggers when we told him we were going to the Bowlingreen army. You would have had light duty with me and plenty of fun with me, and you will find out the difference before many days have passed—They turned us out at Bowlinggreen and we were informed where to find the Kentucky Regiments, so off we started along the railroad line—and to the left of the road we found after going about a mile or so, the camp of the 3rd Kentucky. It was literally but a camp, the regiments were off on a march to Rochester,[30] and only a few invalides and camp gard had been left—Co D was represented in a row of deserted tents all [but] one, into which we anxiuously peered and joined in a little social party enjoying a quiet game of pocher, with corn as markers[.] Ike Kerr, Tom Brown,

29. "Indiana" may have been John W. Bates, who enlisted at Bowling Green on September 30, 1861, in Company A, 4th Kentucky Regiment, and died of wounds suffered at Shiloh on April 7, 1862. *Report of the Adjutant General of the State of Kentucky: Confederate Kentucky Volunteers, War 1861–65* (Frankfort, Ky.: 1915–), 146–47 (hereafter cited as Kentucky Adjutant General Report).

30. Rochester is located on the Green River. In *History of the Orphan Brigade*, we read: "The 2nd Regiment, a company of Tennessee cavalry, and Byrne's Battery . . . were sent forward to Green River, and encamped near the bridge, with a view to its protection and a probable advance . . . the Federals occupying Elizabethtown. The remainder of the brigade, though some of them passed up the road as far as Horse Cave . . . were finally all encamped at Bowling Green . . . the 2nd Regiment stayed at Green Bridge until the first week in October when they moved back to Bowling Green." Henry George, *History of the 3rd, 7th, 8th, and 12th Kentucky, C.S.A.* (Louisville, 1911), 51–52.

Young[31] and others, the three first I remember well as we were afterwards messmates for a long time—I showed them the direction Col. Tyleman gave me, and told them how highly he spoke of the Paducah Co.—You will see them when they come off of the march, and will have to confess you never saw a finer body of men. I asked them many questions, which one accustomed to armies as they are in Europe would—I asked them about the awkward squad drill of which I expected to serve my apprenticeship in at once. Oh! they said it has been too warm for some time to drill, but when it freshens up and the boys all get back you will have plenty of drilling to your hearts content. But talk of drills and camp life you should have seen us at Camp Boon[32]—Poor old Third Kentuck, how you have come down since those days. Then we had no cooking to do, but fine clothes, plenty of good things of all kinds from home, by jove, whole boxes full every day, and a band of music which now has dwindled down to a few tuters, and pretty girls to dance with. [*October*] Oh! get out— those we[re] fine days sure enough,—The camp all beautifully staked out, no piles of rubish as you see now and where you see an old skillet and coffee pot now, which you have to look after all the time to keep from being lifted by your neighbors, we had negroes, each man two and always plenty on hand for any friends coming in—This was the picture of the 3rd Ky as it was compared with what I found it, but even those times were looked back later in the war to as days of luxury and ease—so hard became our sufferings and fastings—I had got up a good appetite [from] my walked and hinted I would like to be iniciated in the art of cooking in the army, and asked if they had regular men detailed as cooks for the army. The[y] laughed at the idea, no—we all cook now we have left good old Camp boon What['s] your name, Chapman, well Chap's or Rome whichever you like best come into our mess, it is the best in the Company, you seem a good

31. J. W. Kerr, T. B. Brown, and (probably) Charles Younger, in George, *History of the 3rd, 7th, 8th, and 12th Kentucky*, 166–67.

32. According to William C. Davis, Camp Boone was located in Montgomery County, Tennessee, seven miles from the county seat of Clarksville, two miles west of the Louisville and Nashville tracks, and just two miles south of the Kentucky border, close enough for Kentuckians to reach in order to enlist and in a place where Kentucky's neutrality would not be violated. Established in July 1861, it was named for Daniel Boone. William C. Davis, *The Orphan Brigade: The Kentucky Confederates Who Couldn't Go Home* (Garden City, N.Y.: Doubleday), 13.

enough sort of fellow and we will let you in—This was the rough but hearty welcome I received. And struck out at once with a camp kettle for the spring, as my office was that of water carrier to the mess, a position I held to all through my life in the army—it being often the hardest labor, and yet at the same time the most agreeable, for I have often found after stooping over the fire baking bisquits or frying meat that the taste for what you eat is lost—and as eating is what a soldier principally has to think off, it [is] well to gard as much appetite for a repast at which if you are at all bashful, or feel in the least indisposed there is always some one to look after and make way with your rations, and when your delicate appetite has reached its right pitch, empty plates will be all that will be before you—This lesson I got that very evening, after returning from the spring with my camp kettle full of water, and its full impression of mud on the last civillian pants I wore for many a day afterward—I don't think Indiana liked the chaffing reckless dare devil fellows of the Paducah company, they were up to too many tricks for him—so he already talked of going into another company he liked better, and I forget when we were sworn in if it was in Co. B—or E—that he enlisted in.

After being in the camp a couple of hours an order came from the Lt. Colonel—Colonel Thompson[33]—for us to report up to the Adjutants tent and be sworn in—When Indiana and I went up, the Lt. Col was lying back in state, and the little red bearded adjutant pen in hand ready to make us soldiers of the C.S. It was a proud moment to me when I could stand up and my hand in the air, swair to serve and never desert the Confederate cause so help me God. I felt every inch a man, and a soldier—The Adjutant asked me whether 12 months or three years was the time we wanted to serve and said other regiments from Kentucky are in for 12 months but we went in three years or the war from the start. We put ourselves down for the war as long as it lasted. The Lt. Col a country squire looking sort of a fellow to give grandure to the closing of the scene in a stentorious order [said] that we should be shown to our quarters and have all we required, at the very time he knew there were no blankets any where, and not a very large supply of straw for the night, which after a long hot day as the sun began to sit promised to be a very cold one—I

33. Albert P. Thompson was named lieutenant colonel when the 3d Kentucky was organized in July 1861. George, *History of the 3rd, 7th, 8th, and 12th Kentucky*, 44.

tumbled down in the straw but it was too cool to sleep, and I got up and sat by the camp fire. It was a lovely night. The campfires and the tents all around were new and strange to me, and my position still more so— I wondered where friends I had longed to see in the south were, and whether this cold chilly night they thought of a half Italian who they had last seen in Rome, and who was on their sides, and if fate would ever through me in their path. Who would ever think of me way off in Kentucky— Next day I determined to write to the few friends whose names I remembered, and turned in for the night in the straw again, by keeping close to Indiana I kept warm, I should say from freezing, but as morning drew on it was colder and colder which made me think of the rug I forgot at the shop[?]. I bought it in London. A comrade next to me, who had not known what became after night, through his blanket partly over me, and next morning I found to do so he had exposed himself to the pitterless cold—I had been drilling on board ship with the rest and for fun and found when we had a little practice in the morning, that with what I had picked up by seeing the French and Italians at it in Rome that my Confederate comrades were not far ahead of me, so much so that some began to think I had seen the elephant[34] before in the way of drilling as Indiana had, and was only playing possum. All this I mention as it may have let Lt. Col Thompson to come to the conclusion he did about. Be that as it may be it was in this way that I found out, that by my very act of joining the Southern army at the time and in the company I did, and my whole appearance and bearing of an European, for so help me God I cannot imagine my looking any thing like a Yankey as they afterward told me they did—

After passing [?] the morning writing to Genl Wise, my father, Mr. Rose, Mr. Yeatman[35] and others, I went into town to mail them— As I was posting them in the post office one of my company, told I had better have them countersigned by Colonel Thompson—The moment I was told that I was about to do something out of rule, I started back to camp with my letters—I found the Lt Col in his [illegible] and gave him the letters to countersign. But Sir, they [are]

34. To have "seen the elephant" was to have gained experience or to have seen the world; most important, in the Civil War it meant that one had seen combat. Partridge, *Dictionary of Slang*, 256.

35. Arthur G. Rose was a prominent banker in Charleston, South Carolina, and an old friend of John Gadsby Chapman. The Rose family befriended Chapman during

sealed—I do not countersign sealed letters—And looked at me in a way I shall never forget— He said you are a spie and I mean to find you out—I was so mad I could hardly contain myself, and military life had brought me down to act the part of a marionette. I hardly know what I did I was out of his tent and back in my own in a second with my letter oppened and torn but still clenched in my fist— The poor fellow was a gallant officer, and at Baton Rouge[36] distinguished himeself and was badly wounded and finely was killed in a gallant charge at Paducah at the head of his old Regiment [and?] others which we[re] turned into [a] Cavalry Reght and yet with it all, I cannot ever forget the bitter tears of rage he caused me to shed, as I stood in my tent with my letters in my hand, and sick at heart with every thing. Was it this I had deserted my home to face— A spie, I a spie. I laughed[. H]ow little those that surrounded me knew me— I would show them how much of a spie I was— Never did I ask of that man a favor, and never neglected every salute that was due him—had he have crossed my beat[?] at night I would have shot him, with a grin such as he gave me when I left his tent that afternoon. Long afterwards one day I overheard a conversation between him and Capt Oates[37] at Vicksburg. The Capt was bragging of the Company as usual, and talking in the highest terms of John Garret,[38] who was the best soldier in it. When my vanity was flattered by the Col remarks, which were—You may say what you like about Garret and the others, but if I wanted something done do you know who I would have? Why no other than that little Italian of yours—Which showed me he had changed his idea of my being a spie, but even this [didn't] southe my wounded pride— I mention all this for the last page is a record of my sevearest suffering in the army—which came while yet the flush of sentiment and enthusiasm was on me, and the Paducah Company had no idea of what a proud heart beat under the rough exterior that stood up in their ranks and answered to the name of Chapman at roll call. From that day I sought

---

his later service in Charleston and in Paris and England after the war. The elder Chapman knew Yeatmans in Kentucky, Tennessee, and Mississippi.

36. The Battle of Baton Rouge was fought on August 5, 1862. See Ben L. Bassham, *Conrad Wise Chapman: Artist and Soldier of the Confederacy* (Kent, Ohio: Kent State Univ. Press, 1998), chap. 4, for a discussion of this engagement.

37. S. J. Oates, captain. George, *History of the 3rd, 7th, 8th, and 12th Kentucky*, 166.

38. John Jarret. Ibid., 167.

the acquaintance of no one, and determined to remain with that regiment and company, until no shadow could be cast on my sincerity which I am proud to say I did—

The Regiment at last got back from the march to Rochester— and a hungry tired set of fellows they were after a long march in pursuit of their more light footed enemies who on such occasion in variably show their knowledge of the double double quick, the word skeedadle had not then had its origin, though it ought to have begun with the first Manassas and Bull run— The[y] left the Yanks still running and came back sore footed disgusted and mad with everyone in general, especially with those who had been left behind, and were crowing over their discomfiture by way of making them feel more comfortable— My case was the novelty of the season. Tents have mighty long years, and I got the benefit of them[.] Much to my amusement or rather disgust—One fellow swore he had seen me in Paducah selling Brass Jesuses and plaster casts. Another thought as I was an Italian I must be a barber, and poked his ugly mug in the tent for a shave, I would have cut his d——d throat for him, had he persisted much longer in his importunities. Fellows from other companies flocked to see the showe, the word passed around, Rome where is Rome, Old Rome until it got to be my name in the regiment. Indiana was no longer about. I almost missed him to keep me company, for is not very pleasant to be conspicuous at any time especially in a company, in which you know no one except yourself—

I took it all as good naturedly as I could, for I saw they were a jolly set of fellows after all that I would enjoy to be with— And answered their questions, or feigned ignorance about Rome etc— One asked me what city in Rome did you say you lived in, etc. I answered him, no place of importance only a little two horse town called Italia— That fellow let me alone after that, and when I commenced [to] remind them of what I saw of them when I used to go about selling my brass Jesuses.

I gave the fellow who wanted the shave the last emblem of my office, and let my beard grow—A soldier, a boy of nineteen a pipe in his mouth, and a growing beard, and a little quiet corner in his heart for romance and laurels to win for his mistress— What charming existence to live[.] I look back at those days with the wish that they might have ended there if they could not continue. And yet we know not what we wish— I remember the castles in the air I was building then and I now see how foolish I was, who knows but that my saying now I no longer build them is a proof that I am ——[illegible]—— I stop to think which way I have got way off in Castles in the air, and blush to find the starting point is with my beard—Yes my beard, I thought what a surprise and perhaps a sensation I might make, in the gay uniforms they gave us and brass buttons, and my beard, my first photograph as a soldier— How I used to look at it and smile to think—who would know me as the gay soldier today— Tattered clothes and shoeless feet in a few short months told a different story. Any one who had seen me promenading in Bowlingreen on Sundays after church with a rose bud in my button hole that some pretty Kentucky girl had put there, and my cap cocked on one side would never [have] recognized in the neglected dusty dirty shabby lazzaroni[39] looking individual in rags with a black pipe in his mouth and a riddled slouched hat covering his eyes as one and the same—

But back again to Bowling green and let us leave until later the life of the 3d Ky in the swamps of Louisiana and Mississippi—

To think of the thousand insidents of the camp life at Bowlingreen alone and record them all would be an endless undertaking. Not a day passed but some new story went the rounds of camp— and died at night a new one taking its start from groups of the old third around their camp fires— As the Paducah Company marched into camps from their Rochester march, they were indeed to be re-marked by their soldierly bearing, and at the same time you could see they were gentlemen almost to a man— They stacked their guns and prepared to cook something for their evening supper— The next day was a day of rest for them, and stretched in their blankets they enjoyed a days nap in the sun which was quite comfortable at this season— Johnny Rochel[40] who was one of my mess mates, knew and was known to every body and a queer genius in his way—Fond of his little game of pocher and seven up, and never had any compunctions of conscience about stacking four aces for himself and four kings for his partner, and turning up the Jack from the bottom of the stack when he wanted one point at old sledge[41]— He was

39. A *lazzarono* (plural *lazzaroni*) is a rascal or good-for-nothing.

40. John Rochelle. George, *History of the 3rd, 7th, 8th, and 12th Kentucky,* 167.

41. "Old sledge" was a card game also known as "all fours," "pitch," and "seven-up." To "study the history of the four kings" was to play cards. Partridge, *Dictionary of Slang,* 393.

unprincipled in many things but on the whole a good soldier, and a capital cook, every body knew his and Bill Lamdens tricks. I mention them first as the two scape graces[42] of the Company. Bill Lamden[43] would stop at nothing and you to keep himself in practice in the art of picking pockets by practicing on some of the Com—who generally gave him more than he bargained for. He was dirty in his stealing, whereas Rochel never stooped to small matters, but when a side of bacon or a bag of coffee was to be confiscated from the Comesary he was always in command of the storming party— He was generous reckless, never paid his debts a hard case every way, and he it was who came forward and met me more cordially than any of the rest. A runaway himself and cast off by his family and friends who were in a good position in New Orleans, and no longer recognized the Mississippi steamboat adventurer who went down from bad to worse when the war commenced[. H]e was found behind a bar in Paducah[.] Bill Lamden was his menial in subjection and in terror— Dick Turpen[44] were the names they went by.

Otto F. Rosencrantz and Bob Beard[45] were my two best friends in the Co., both messmates. Rosencrantz was a boy 13 or fourteen years old, the youngest soldier in the Co.—At the beginning of the war he was at school and ran away from his father who was a brother of the Yankey General and shared his ultra radical opinions—He was anxious to get his runaway boy back again, and begged threatened and tryed to persuade him to return, and finally sent a substitute for him, with a request to the Col of the regt to start his son back to Paducah. The sharp little fellow got the substitute sworn in and thanked his father for sending an other soldier to the Confederacy.

42. "Scape graces" are unprincipled nor incorrigible people who have "[e]scaped grace."

43. Probably W. F. Lambdin. George, *History of the 3rd, 7th, 8th, and 12th Kentucky*, 167.

44. Neither a "Dick Turpen" nor any name resembling that appears in the muster rolls of the "Orphan Brigade."

45. Otto F. Rosencrantz and R. M. Baird. George, *History of the 3rd, 7th, 8th, and 12th Kentucky*, 166. Otto and William Starke Rosecrans (1819–1898), the Union general from Ohio, were undoubtedly both descendants of Harmon Hendrik Rosenkrantz, who arrived in New Amsterdam in 1651. The general's grandfather changed the name to Rosecrans during the American Revolution to avoid being taken for a Hessian. See William M. Lamers, *The Edge of Glory: A Biography of William S. Rosecrans* (New York: Harcourt, Brace & World, 1961).

The Col nor Capt any how had no hold on him as he was much below the age for the army and could leave any day he thought fit. But the galant little fellow held on the last, and in each battle distinguished by his bravery, and almost foolhardy recklessness sometimes[.] [*Facing page:* Rosencrantz died in Paducah at his home from his wounds after the war was over—]

Bob Beard, was a character for any novelist to study— Thackery or Dickens might search the world over without finding such an other—He could play old soldier[46] better than any one I ever saw undertake the part. He managed never to be on guard of a cold night and if he was it was always at some comfortable post with a good fire, he would go around and be sure of the number of the centinel at the Comisary, which was generally the last, when you would see old Bob just about guard mounting time hunting here for his gun and there for his cartridge box and when all had fallen in and been numbered you would see him striking across the field in great haste buckling on his traps and swearing at the boys for meddling with his accoutrements[.] If you happened to see him on post, quietly seated on a stump by a good fire reading the newspaper of which he always carried a provision sometimes they were several months old but always of the same interest to him. Hellow Old Diobetes was our usual salute to him. D[amn] you old [soul?] how did you get this easy place[.] A grin from him would follow each word as he would say you must learn to be old soldiers if you want to reap their reward— Another reason for his fondness for the duty of guarding the Comisary in the time that coffee used to be had, was that he always liked his remarkably strong and he being in our mess we were not sorry of the little supply we found on hand after his guard duty. Of course no one out of the mess was let in to the secret and we all joined the corus of curses on all comisaries and short rations of everything and were particularly fearce [on?] the coffee question. The way he got his Soubriquet was that he professed always to have this malady when long marches or drills were expected and generally got off as he always had a canteen of whiskey to get into the good graces of the surgeon with, and wink at the boys on a march quietly pearched on

46. An "old soldier" is an experienced, crafty man. In Civil War slang an "old soldier" was adept at devising ways of avoiding routine tasks. Partridge, *Dictionary of Slang*, 586.

the top of some wagon while the rest of us were tramping up to our eyes in mud. Go in glory, boys, give us your gun old Ike I will carry it for you awhile you look played out. Hellow my little Roman, how do you like the fun, don't you wish yourself in Rome again. The Colonel would come along, Oh theres Bob, yes Col, won't you have a drink I got some real old rie[.] A word for every one, and a show of his splendid [illegible] and a grin he would give you and I['d] be hanged if any one could look grim and look Bob full in his handsome face any time. He held the same position in the mess that I did, that of water carrier, and I would have been very sorry to have seen him replaced by any one else although of a morning I had to be very sharp, if I did not want my usual lot of toating the heavy bucket to the spring while he loafed along with the coffee pot and our apparatus for the morning toilet in the branch close by. In my whole experience in the army I never met a more social and agreeable messmate[.] Good old Bob, with all your faults I defie any one to dislike you— I shall remember you all my life, and often look back to our campaigning together—With all his old soldiering Bob was no shirk—When the time came of the fight and you saw what every man in the company is made of, he was always at his post to do or die— Though before and after the fight he would invariably talk of his inclination to run— These two Rosencrantz and Bob Beard were my two most intimate comrades in the Company— Ike Kerr filled the place of cook, a tinner by trade an a good natured well disposed fellow— He was nicknamed Sibley[47] from the shape of his hat which had been used to hold water so often that it became the shape of a funnel, and the various uses that this article was put to, such as dusting the ashes out of skilets and as a guard against hot handles, etc., made it useful as well as ornamental— Young of German decent was second in that Department and made the fires Rosencrantz attended to the frying of the meat. Tom Brown the lazy drummer of the Co. made the Coffee. Bob and I were the water toaters, and Johnny Rochel the bully and head of the mess and was always ready to stand up for mess no 1 and a gay one it was while it lasted. It was however but of short duration changes were made after each move of the army or a fight.

47. The Sibley tent, invented by Henry Hopkins Sibley, was conical in shape and supported by a single pole; it could accommodate about twelve soldiers. Boatner, *Civil War Dictionary*, 760.

My first month of camp life past monotously by[. N]o incident
marked the course of the beginning of my soldier life. Every day I
felt myself more and more the reckless careless devil of a soldier,
which do what I ever will in life I shall always be. My character was
formed in the armies of the south and for better or worse I must
abide by it. After reveille the days routine was early drill in the man-
ual of arms before breakfast— a breakfast of coffee and bisquits anything but light although yellow with soda which was put in with the
intention of making them so— a few slices of fryed bacon, a good
appetite soon dispatched, and we were ready for a snooze in the sun,
or at least those who [had] the shaded corner in a tent or under a
tree and the study of the history of the four kings did not afford
greater attractions[.] At times like these my pencil would be of use,
and all the groups were recorded at the time with a daily journal of
my life which is now in other hands or I might have no occasion for
writing the present one— When in the afternoon about two there
was no Brigade drill, Ben Anderson[48] our major then, used to have
us out in an old field near camp, where he would put us through all
the evolutions of the line, and we returned to camp at a double quick
to get dinner— Sometimes we had old Ike excused and found our
meal ready and had time to devour it before dress parade—, and if
dress was what was aimed at no parade was ever more miscalled—
Dress circles at the opera, are supposed to be uniform, and at that
time a great variety was to be seen in the gallant 3d Ky. It was dress
up you fellow in the brown jeans and keep your gun at a support
until you are ordered you there with [the] yellow shirt—Every variety from the Backwoodsman blouse to the dandy State guards uniform and the country squire's dress and the city naybob, some with
old flint-locks[.] I remember mine was such, other[s] their shot guns
and others whose time of service in Yankee hands had expired with
their owners— The End of the day was this grand Parade. Attention to orders Orderly sargents to the front Capt. officer of the day
Lt officer of the guard, in those days we had three or four tuters
which constituted our band and marched up and down our line. After this we doubled quick back to camp, put away our arms for the
day, cooked our supper and passed our night, long after roll call and

48. Benjamin Anderson became a major upon the organization of the 3d Kentucky and later was promoted to lieutenant colonel. George, *History of the 3rd, 7th,
8th, and 12th Kentucky*, 44, 163.

An 1867 etching by Chapman entitled *Camp Scenes.* Courtesy of the
Valentine Museum, Richmond.

taps chatting by the camp fires. Lights had all to be out by taps but althrough camp any one anxious to find out if orders were carried strickly out would have found many a party still using the history of the kings although the small hours of the morning were on them, and one tallow candle after another had succeeded each other in the bayonet stuck in the ground as a candlestick, whose raise were carefully screened from regimental Hd Quarters by a barril, a box or anything—in the way— I doubt myself if anything would have been needed at this time for Tylmann the disciplinarian was away, and Col Tompson and Ben Anderson, were probably at the same business themselves— While pocker seven up and Yucka[49] were going on, and confederate notes and silver went the rounds and fell to the most lucky and some times to the most skillful in the art of taking in his adversary, a few of us recounted what little experience we had had in life before joining the army, a gay song, or ritch story enlivened the hours as they passed, Leon[50] would get out his violin and play for us and when he did and I could shut out from around me the scene, of a boisterous camp and listen and forget where I was, I would dream over dreams that I thought a soldiers life had hardened me against forever— I would forget the reality of the drill next morning, my turn on guard, and think of a life such if I had had a chance such as many have had, I came back to my stumpy black pipe again which had gone out while my thoughts traveled many a mile and brushed a way a tear which none had seen, and tried to laugh at myself for my foolishness. It is strange that through life music always has a great effect on me, and I have not the power of repeating a single tune— I shall never forget when after long persuasion Leon undertook to put an old camp fiddle in tune, and the echoes he woke up in the forest that night. He was an accomplished musician— We grew to be strong friends— His life had been an adventurous one from Boyhood he left Ireland and had wandered through America ever since. He was a thorough Gent in every respect and a brave soldier—and has done me many a kind turn, but for none I thank him more than for have awakened me from the

49. "Yucka" is Chapman's creative spelling of eucre, a popular card game.
50. There was a J. H. Keon in Company D who rose to the rank of 3d lieutenant. It is not possible to know if there was a "Leon," since most enlisted men are listed on muster rolls by last names and first initials only. George, *History of the 3rd, 7th, 8th, and 12th Kentucky*, 166.

brutal selphish existence which a soldier soon falls into and which if he cannot keep his personal character throuout he will soon be molded into the machine, which it takes not long to make, but which is for ever worthless for nought else except the marrionet[.]

Tom Ewell was a queer case sure enough, a real specimen of a Southern country lad, with his coon skin cap drawn down over his years, his head bent forward, walking as if he was following some trail all the time. You scarcely ever saw him smile, but when he did it was a most pleasing one and lit up his whole face, which at all other times was that of a morose discontented soldier— So famous for insatiable appetite did he become that although a hard worker in a mess, he could persuade but few of his being an acquisition to one— He never growled on duty of any kind that he was ordered to perform, and did it always with a vim, at work on fortifications while others would play off he was at the mark pick or shovel in hand— If one of his mess were on guard and could not come in for their meals, they were sure of having their portion saved[.] The reason perhaps why we never met in a mess, was that I shared an almost equal reputation for being a good eater, with the disadvantage of being but and indifferent worker, which were by no means good recommendations to get in a mess. Perhaps it was better as it was, for together we might have bred a famine. Tom Ewell, every one felt that they did not know you, and I as little as the next although you were my own cousin as I soon found out.[51] In a battle you were always seen following up the trail the Yankey generally left behind them of knapsacks and accoutrements, just as you would some bear in your Ky mountains, perhaps, and never look back until you got him in a hole unless ordered to desist— You forgot no doubt on such occasion every thing but your game, and your comrades found out, although a man of few words, and a hard eater, you could show some of them something in the hunting line at least which might be of service to them—

Sam Gohegan[52] who did not know old Sam— We called him old on account of his white hear, but there were older koons in the Company, but more artful ones I defie you to find anywhere— Sam was

51. Conrad's great-grandfather on his father's side, Thomas Chapman, married Susanna Ewell, daughter of Maj. Bertrand Ewell of Prince William County, Virginia. Horace E. Hayden, *Virginia Genealogies* (Wilkes-Barre, Pa.: Genealogical Publishing Co., 1891), 335–37.

52. Samuel Geoghegan. George, *History of the 3rd, 7th, 8th, and 12th Kentucky*, 167.

not over forty and a good marcher, and a trump of a fellow in a fight, and as jolly as you please on a spree. He would take many a drink before being muddled and many a ritch story would follow. Old Sam gave us the slip to join Morgan[53] and we never heard more of him— Irishman like he was always ready for a fight, and though often underguard no one could hold a grudg against him long— I should have put you in the head of the list in the company, you and George Harden[54] with all his dislike to minnie balls, and his preference for the quiet post in the Comisary, always stood up for the Paducah boys, in spight of our lifting whole sides of bacon from his lardory, which he had to account for in some way. He had to bear the suspicions of his chief of having used them either to greaze his belly or his boots— Yes his boots— But first I must state that said George Harden was in a Brigade of tall men the tallest—7 feet at least in his boots—a propos de bottes—at roll call one of those frosty cold mornings in december he was in great haste he reached for his boots to answer to his name, when horrors, they were frozen as hard as rocks, what could he do but rip them up in every direction and when he said Here, some one sang out George Harden has cut his boots. George looked mad, and this was the starting point of what caused many a quarrel between George and the Co— From Company to Co—it soon spread—[I]t reached other regts and where ever he showed himself he was presented with George show us where you cut your boots. One fellow way off would sing out Hellow Paduc what's the news. Why George Harden has cut his boots— It became a [illegible] worse than Lambor[?]—and was shouted from regt to regt—to his greatest disgust—so much so that he left the company and took to cutting up meet— At Shiloh I believe he fought well, but as he did take an other [illegible] we all thought he liked the Comisary better— Come up Co. D and draw your rations—Is that all the sugar

53. John Hunt Morgan (1825–1864) was one of the Civil War's most colorful characters. Commissioned a captain and given command of a squadron of cavalry in 1861, he was promoted to colonel and led the Kentucky squadron of cavalry at Shiloh. After rising to brigadier general and head of a division, he was captured at New Lisbon, Ohio, and held prisoner at the state penitentiary in Columbus before making a daring escape. He was killed in September 1864 at Greenville, Tennessee. Boatner, *Civil War Dictionary,* 566.

54. George "Harden" was probably G. O. Heyden, 5th sergeant. George, *History of the 3rd, 7th, 8th, and 12th Kentucky,* 166.

you drew for 80 men (we drew rations for more men always than we had in camp) and that side of bacon there ought to come to us, there George throw in that for us and come around to supper at your mess— Don't give me all bone. Look at George saving the tit bits for his mess. Take your meat and get out of my way, and he would shake his giant form and flourish his big knife, which every body knew would never cut anything intentionally except the grub he issued— If you forgive me old George for the sketch I made of you and your boots and sent to the Louisville Journal, and the sides of bacon and haversack of coffee I help[ed] to dispose of I will forget your falts and put you down in my next picture making love to a pretty girl which I know is bound to please you[.]

Our battalion drills were generally commanded by Ben Anderson— Our brigade and Division drills by Buckner and Breckenridge.[55] Buckner was a tough old fellow at a sham fight and used to manage us splendidly—Cavalry infantry and artillery the cavalry charging our squares, and I never realized the tamness of this parade[?] until I got hold of the reality— Little Sargt Thomas[56] got the devil from Buckner one day for not coming up in time as left guide and we joked him about it for ever afterwards— Breckenridge you could see had had but little practice by this mode of drilling— He was a splendid man in every respect and we all soon [came] to love him as a father— At our grand reviews which took place principally on Mondays, Genl Albert Sidney Johnson[57] always was present, and his imposing look as he rode along our line, his eye seemed

55. Simon Bolivar Buckner (1823–1914), a Kentuckian who had been offered commissions in both the Union and Confederate armies early in the conflict, was appointed brigadier general by Johnston in September 1861. He surrendered Fort Donelson to his old friend Grant. Exchanged in August 1862, he fought at Chattanooga, Perryville, and Chickamauga. After the war he served as governor of Kentucky and resumed his friendship with Grant. John C. Breckenridge (1821–1875), also from Kentucky, served in the U.S. Congress and as vice president under Buchanan. He ran for president in 1860 and subsequently became a U.S. senator. He was appointed brigadier general in November 1861. After Appomattox he fled the United States and lived abroad until a general amnesty was declared in 1869. Boatner, *Civil War Dictionary*, 95–96, 82–83.

56. F. W. Thomas, 1st sergeant. George, *History of the 3rd, 7th, 8th, and 12th Kentucky*, 166.

57. Gen. Albert Sidney Johnston (1803–1862), commanding general of the Western Department (Confederate armies between the Alleghenies and the Mississippi), died of a leg wound at Shiloh on April 6. Boatner, *Civil War Dictionary*, 440.

to be riveted on every man as he slowly rode by, and had a great effect— He had a severe look always, but appeared so thoroughly a
soldier that it would have been strange had he looked otherwise[.]
The people of Bowling green thought he had over a hundred thousand men within [the] neighborhood[.] And these displays were well
calculated to have that effect, for we often wondered in our ignorance why we were always reviewed at different points, changed camp
so often, and when we went out on a march, always came back on the
trains and vice versa—Hard days of work on fortifications but the
sand ones and where we had to content against the hard rock of the
mountains— I worked as hard as I knew how, but often at first covered myself more with the dirt I was digging and I through out of
the ditch with my spade At the rock business I succeeded better for
after a blast I could use the pick tolerably well— and through out
the fragments with my hands— The only day I remember having
played truant was when I was put on extra duty, and ought to have
been made to work for my failure to be at roll call at the proper
time—

Three of us one morning thought we would exchange the mo-
notony of camp life for a ramble in the country, and as strict orders
were that no one should leave camp except to go to the spring, we
each armed ourselves with a bucket or coffee pot and put off after
our mornings breakfast, after having hid our passes in some bushes
near camp to answer the purpose of returning we then were at liberty to enjoy the delightful sensation of being away from camp against
orders, and kick our heels in freedom of the orderly sargent of the
day. We had a feast on Hazel nuts, apples and persimmons which I
learned from experience were not to be eaten when too temptingly
looking, and only the wilted ones were good. Now Rome pitch in
and get your persimmons, the red ones are the best, I tried one which
drew my mouth up, to [the] width it ought naturally to have been,
and could not soon them for the sell—

We wandered thus many miles from camp and lunched outside
of our lines—with some butter milk we got at a house, which before
entering we armed ourselves with rocks, to defend ourselves if there
was a fray— but soon chucked the[m] away as the old lady bid us
welcome, and told us to help ourselves in the oarcherd which we
intended any how to do— When we got back to camp it was late at
night, roll call had been called, and we had been marked absent from

morning drill and dress parade and also roll call— and placed on the list of extra duty for the next day— The feast we sent in to the Capt and gave the different boys in the company did not mitigate our sentence as in fact we knew the rules of the Co— sufficiently to know it would not and next day we were marched up to work[.] I was mad at being obliged to do that which I gladly of as usual duty or as a volunteer, but this day they should not have the benefit of my services, so I hunted up a quiet place behind a rock, and my sketch book and haversack with the remains of our day befores plunder received my attentions for the rest of the day— and I returned to camp satisfied that at least extra duty had not got me that once, although I richly deserved it. This was the first and only time in the army I was punished, and the lesson was a good one not to transgress for the future which my pride prevented me from ever doing again—

The Company at that time was commanded by Capt Solms, next as the roll call ran Lt Ellis, Lt Kinkade Lt Otes then Sargt Turk etc. and so on—from Alderson down to W. W. Wilson[58] who was last on the list— To attempt to describe the different members of the company, as I once readily did while writing my first memoranda of camp life the task being easier as having the originals before [me.] I had but to take their likeness before each name as they came on the list— I shall confine myself to the description of the first and the last on the roll. Alderson—or Avelanche as we called, from the fact of his always called Ambulances by that name, was a tall lean Virginian, as witty a fellow as you could find any where, and with a knowing wink in the eye that spoke volumes, always in a good humour, and a capital fellow to be on guard with. W. W. Wilson was just his opposite in appearance, a fat beefy muddled headed, good hearted boy, just another boy, as Dickens has in his Pickwick papers[59]— If you were sick he would be the first to look out for you, or if your mess forgot you at mess time, he would always get you something from the Capts or the Col's cooks with all of which he was good friends and there was no one like Mas[?] Wilson—My old

58. Oscar J. Sonies, captain; Powhatan Ellis, 1st lieutenant; Milton Kinkead, 2d lieutenant; S. J. Oates, 2d lieutenant; James A. Turk, 3d sergeant; J. H. Alderson; and W. W. Wilson. George, *History of the 3rd, 7th, 8th, and 12th Kentucky*, 166–67.

59. Conrad is referring to a character known simply as "The Fat Boy" in Dickens's novel.

Paducah Co—what changes you have undergone since those days, many whose names I have recorded have passed away forever. And to record the untimely end of these brave fellows would be too sad a task and I shrink from it, my own is sad enough without it. And those who have died on the battle field, unconscious of the end, we who survive them have witnessed—It is hard to say which are to be the most pitied— [*November 1861*] We live, we eat, sleep and life passes on, if they envy us, I can't say much for their present abode poor fellows— We who are left, have a sacred duty to perform, that is to keep them in remembrance and and the wrongs to avenge which they died for, to be worthy of them. I believe every Confederate soldier ought to remember that he is such and abide his time when he can when the roll is called, fall into his old place, or answer—to another roll call if it is ever held— Paducah Rats— I first learned to be a soldier in your midst, the school was a hard one, but it made many a man, that otherwise might have never found out what he was put in the world for beyond [to] have his own ease and comfort— Not one that I know of in the Company, but when I left them was not sorry to see me go[.] And their is no greater pleasure and satisfaction of pride to a soldiers, than to know that his comrades, who were when he met them but strangers to him, at his departure such true and staunch friends—

But to get back to Bowlingreen in November December and January— and the few incident[s] worth recording there, it will take but a few pages more— A month had passed, and no excitement of any kind had disturbed the monotous calm of camp life, when one night, after taps a report came into camp that our pickets and outposts had been driven in by Yankey cavalry and a call for reinforcements. This was just the duty I was glad to get and I hasten to volunteer my services— With a good supply of ammunition and our guns ready for use, and a hunter a head of our little party to guide the way through the dark stormy night I thought as we climbed up the mountain side, what a picture it would have made our arrival at the Hd Qurts of our pickets, our lantern lighting up the groups on the ground, and the glimmer of a second showing itself through the bushes where the Lt. of the guard had his quarters, in a crevice in some rocks— Well boys he said we shall have work probably before morning— And away we started to reinforce the different posts. If I remember right Cob[60] was my partner on duty. It was a dark night, and we had orders to fire after the first challenge, and our guns were leveled down the path, hours passed and so great was the excitement of anxious expectations, that they passed by without our knowing that we had been on for four instead of two— It was my first duty as picket and I kept as good a watch as if I could see the whole Yankey, where I saw but one mass of black, no trees nothing, even my partner on duty I could only tell when he was near by a touch. When we were relieved and turned in for the night on a flat rock with our cartridge boxes for pillows it began to rain, such a rain I thought then I had never felt before, in that way I certainly never had, I was soon drenched to the skin, and the only dry place I could find I had secured for the lock of my gun— at day brake it still poared, and as none of [the] posts had been disturbed in the night, a party headed by Lt Timberlick[61] proposed a reconaisance, with those of the pickets who had been driven in the previous day from a house by the now distant Yankey cavalry—, and find out there where abouts at the present— So we picked out as many dry cartridges as could be found in the crowd— and moved off in order with an advanced guard etc.— We had not broken our fast and what with the rain and a sleepless night did not feel very flush— It was my first turn out of the kind and my novel positions was exciting— We moved along the road cautiously and after a long morning walk through the mud reached the little Ky home where the chase had taken place from— We surrounded the house so that no one could escape, and a party went in, I was amongst them— we found an old lady busily engaged making breakfast for her old man, and everything looked peaceful and quiet, quite the opposite from what we were led to expect. When the parties who had been chased recounted their story in the true light the whole affair appeared clear enough— It seems there three or four left the Hd. Quarters of the pickets against orders in search of buttermilk and other luxuries which every soldier is willing to risk the chance of being put in the guard house to secure— They had got what they wanted and were hurrying back to their duty, when some Texican Rangers, coming up to the house which they had just left, were told by the old man that they had just got some

60. There were a number of "Cobbs" in the Orphan Brigade, but no one with that name was in Company D or the 3d Regiment.

61. George W. Timberlake, 1st lieutenant, Company B, 3d Kentucky Regiment. George, *History of the 3rd, 7th, 8th, and 12th Kentucky,* 164.

buttermilk from them and belonged to the Ky Bri. At once they proposed a lark and started off in full tilt the whole party of them after the butter milk rangers, and most probably the Yankey Jackets and overcoats of some of them had got in their frolicks with the Yankees were the cause of the blunder and a wakeful night from us— This was all we gained for our long walk, except a few corn dodgers we shared amongst us on our way back— We often stopped to rest and wondered how we had come so far in so short a time, at last we saw once more our tents looming up in the distance and the cheerful look of campfires was pleasant indeed to a wet tired and hungry soldier— The inside of our tent never had looked as comfortable, and as I stood up before the sparkling fires, for we all had chilmnays to our tents, and got dry clothes on and a comfortable meal which Ike had put aside for me, and my old black pipe and some tobacco dried on the end of a stick— Our expedition had turned out a fiasco but at least I had had the excitement of it, and now enjoyed the delightful sensation of a tired man at rest— This was my first picket, and the first insight I had of the long life of the kind I was soon destined to experience—

Our march to Rochester and back was an other bootless expedition but at least one that the whole brigade was engaged in— We started one cold morning with Genl Breckenridge in Command— Morgans cavalry was with us and Lyons[62] battery— It is a long time ago and I do not remember who else— We passed through Russell-ville famous for pretty girls, and hospitable farmers. At Shakertown[63] we were halted to await Morgan and his Merry men. As they came up and hastened to the front of our column, they presented a very picturesque appearance on their splendid blooded horses all armed with sharps rifles[64] and equipped in splendid style— their horses prancing and their jokes for their old cronies in the web footed cav-

62. H.B. Lyon, *Davis*, 38.

63. "Shakertown" is South Union, Kentucky, located about twelve miles south-west of Bowling Green. There are now a museum and several other original buildings at this crossroads, which still appears much as Chapman would have seen it in 1861.

64. The Sharp (or "Sharp's") rifle was an early breech-loading rifle purchased by the Confederates in 1861 and subsequently manufactured in the South. It could be fired up to ten rounds per minute, three times faster than muzzle-loaders. Boatner, *Civil War Dictionary*, 735–36.

alry was highly amusing. Morgan called out old Sam Gohegan, and gave him a pull out of his canteen, Genl Breckenridge was close by and looked as if he would not have minded to have been in old Sams place, as he smacked his lips and touched his hat to his old friend and fell back in ranks— One horse was particularly lively and I remember at a word from his master would stand up on his hind quarters and attack any horse he was put to— The Shakers looked out of their neat lonesome looking houses half scared of our fun— Some pretty Shaker girls seemed to be more pleased with our jolly troop than the rest, and did not run in at [but?] demonstrated [their?] admiration by kissing our hands, and the little dears looked so actually pleased, that a party went back from our camp that afternoon to see again these fair daughters of Eve, and returned with loads of fine pipin[65] apples and some most incredible stories of the affability of the whole of Shakerdom, and talked (after the war) of settling amongst them. When we reached Rochester, there was not a sign of a Yankey— I believe Morgans men got the only shots that were to be had at the flying foe— An old Yankey jew suttler was all [that was] left in the town, who had a good supply of boots on hand which was a God send to us— Cob of our Company got a couple of bags full— The weather was clear sharp and cold, just the weather for marching— on our return we had no such luck—, the inclement season set in and such mud and mire I had never seen, up to our eyes in mud and the rain coming down, everything wet, the flower, the sugar every thing of the mess— nothing to be cooked and plenty of cursing and swearing against the Comisary, who sometimes would not issue our rations until after his supper about 10- P.M. Well might they say that the tribe after making themselves comfortable study how uncomfortable they can make every one else. A raw turnip would be all we would have until night, and but for an occasional glass of persimmon bear or hard cider I don't know how we would have fared— When ever we halted near a patch of turnips, the order of the charge on the patch, was step in boys and draw you[r] turnips. Having secured a supply in the scramble, I sat on an old broken down fence to enjoy my meal, a fellow soldier sat by me and while thus, we discussed various subjects, but what put me to musing, more

65. A vague reference, "pipin apples" could refer to any of several varieties of apples.

than anything else was one of his remarks, what do you think they say to such a figure as you are in Rome. How they would have laughed to have seen me, I thought, there was not much in my looks to denote anything of the Paino[66] of Rome, and if I had ever dreamed of soldier life as anything very romantic the stern reality of that moment must have cancelled it forever—

One day we were all over our camp fires after a long march from day light, when the whole camp was aroused by one a row in the fourth and as we crowded to see what it was, saw a poor fellow drop down and the terrible wound he had received in the stomach had left him a few minutes to live He was acting as a mediator between two of his Comrades who had a quarel, when he received the blow intended for the man he had wanted to save— It happened thus—At guard mounting one of these men had been detailed as coporal and being a back woods man and little used to military routine when he had to give the order 3d releif right wheel, said 3d coporal right wheel his companions jocked a great deal about it, and with the regt it became as great a see [?] as George Hardens boots, only the other did not take the joke and swore he would kill the next man that insulted him about it. He was in a bad humour on this occasion, when his messmate tantalized him about it, he at once started in to get his gun and came at a charge with his bayonet on the offender, who drew his heavy knife stooped and made a dash at him with his head down, the poor unfortunate mediator stepped between and met with a death he little merited. This was the first tragedy I was a witness to in Camp and it made a great impression on me— That night was a frightfully stormy one. I remember I woke up in the middle of it all, with the wet tent on my face and found myself lying in a regular stream of water which was running down the side of the hill where we had unknowingly pitched it— I felt for my shoes and found them too full of water— I was in a plight sure enough and may well have said what Johnny Rochel and the rest attibuted to me— "Oh my! ain't I in a fix and my shoes a perfect lake"—Wilson that boy of ill luck had knocked over the pole from the tripod that supported our Sibley tent, and scared out of his wits at George Harden who was

66. *Paino* is an archaic Italian term for a dandy, a fop, a gallant, or a "fine gentleman."

swearing he would eat him dead or alive scampered off and left us — while he and the rest were laughing at our difficulty. How it rained as Rosencranz and I gathered up our blankets as best we could and tried to gain admittance in some other tent — but useless our efforts were, all were full— a flicker of light came from a log cabbin close by which was used by the Dr and Comisary, and for it we started determined to get under shelter some where— When we got in and crouched down by the fire to warm ourselves and survey the premises the scene presented a curious one. On one side lay the Dr the Col and Majr on the others the negroe cooks and in the midst of all the corpse of the days tragedy, to complete the melange to privates had come in besides me and stretched out in the only space left between the fire and the corpse and slept sound the remainder of the night— In the morning the Col was looking around for one of his boots and swearing against the whole Kentucky brigade especially the rascally soldiers, who came in everywhere. It was still dark and he had to strike a light, which revealed me and on his stirring me up, also his missing boot.

Our march back to Bowling green was a tedious one as are generally all retrograde movements—At last we reached our old camp and retired to the woods for the winter, where we started to build our log cabbins, which however we were not destined to winter in— The forest rang with the blows of the axx and tree after tree was felled for the purpose of building. After several attempts on my part at this business, I was forced to give up in despair, as my blows were ineffectual compared to the more experienced, and was glad to escape with a gash through my thick shoes and a scratch on my foot for a remembrance, and had to fall in as a toater of logs some of which it almost broke my back to carry. Two of us one day had hold of one of [the] foundation logs, which we were taking to its destination, when Rosencrantz added his wait to the load and we all came down with a crash. Just when we had our cabbins ready and thought we would enjoy the luxury our labours had afforded us— orders came for a move and away we went again—March after march succeeded this move first forward and all hearts would beat with the excitement of pressing forward on Louisville[.] Ben Anderson cheered us on, boys we may be at the Galt House for Christmas yet—he would say—

Those marches what terrible long ones some of them were, and for no apparent purpose, we would march three or four days in succession and then turned back on our tracks weary and soar footed to be once more where we started from— On on occasion we were within a mile of the famous Mamoth Cave[67] and our curiosity was not allowed to be satisfied by a visit to it— Some of the officers went but what business had we to think of going— They were right and we wrong of course— During these marches I have laid out on the ground on a wet blanket which I had wrung before spreading for the night, and which only answered the purpose of absorbing the moisture of the spungy ground it was spread on and was a barrier between it and our skins until sleep would do the rest and at morning awake to find ourselves [illegible] in water— At other times when no trees or bark could be got at, we would cock a couple of rails up agains the fence, spread our blankets on them and turn in for the night, with the comfortable feeling of being safe from the water bubbling along beneath us— Sometimes a frost would come on and beard and blanket were fast frozen together by morning— Dear old Breckenridge never forgot his men on occasions like this and often sent miles to get us a dram to take before turning in and I believe by it he saved more lives than others more cautious about liquor— On the first march of this kind we had tents but could only used them after thawing them near the fire, and sometimes cooking apparatus tents every thing in fact in the wagans were one mass of icicles—After a march of this kind and no suppers it was by no means fun to be sent several miles off on a picket and return in time in the morning to learn that all were on the move, and the third taking the lead on the march—and we destined to [*December 1861*] serve out the rest of our time as the rear guard, helping wagons out of mudholes and ourselves into them— Breckenridge was always along to give a cheering word and sometimes an appropriate joke. They were getting us in order for greater trials that were to follow— Night[s] like these who could wonder at our preferring the rails for to make our fires to the green wood to be cut by night and such nights. I remember however the General coming up with his staff at one of our charges on a fence, and ordered us to put up the rails at once and go and cut

67. Mammoth Cave, today a national park about twenty-five miles northwest of Bowling Green, has long been famous for its limestone caverns.

our wood, which however we were soldiers enough to obey and disobey and as soon as he and his staff turned their backs— A hay stack what a luxury on nights like this each man would start out to get what he could carry for his bed and those who had calculated on making the stack their roost for the night were awfully disappointed when they began to see the stack dwindle to one armful to a man— Farmers raved at the vandal soldiers burning rails and using up their straw, but the requisite had to be supplied— Chap where shall we make our bed, was Rosencranz first question on reaching camp and our blankets were put down to secure the place, fellows claimed any spot they could sellect after leaving their hat or canteen to mark the spot, while other[s] presume to lay claims to spots they had decided on without any such mark of possession— It may seem strange that men should be so childish about a place to sleep on, but amongst soldiers some soon get to be selfish, and would rather have a partner grumbling at the uneven ground and protruding stump and roots under his blanket, than have to sleep under such difficulties one's self— Rosencranz and I each had a blanket and any third one of the party who would join us we would place two blankets down to sleep on to keep out the wet, and lying spoon fashion close together and an other to cover with keep warm all night. It was always preferable to sleep in the middle for you were then sure of having your portion of the blanket undisputed—

Christmas my first away from home, found us camped near our old ground at Bowling green after several bootless expeditions like the Rochester affair— Once more we settled in our tents with chilmneys, which made up for the loss of our cabins which other regiments occupied in our place, and no doubt thanked us for our forethought in building them for them. I feel mortified that in recording this Christmas day, I can say but little to my credit on that eventful day in camp— What happened however may have been for the best, as had it been otherwise in the excitement of the times I might have shared in some of the carrying on— It was a dark cold damp morning, when after the usual roll call, a dram of whiskey was issued to each man, I gulped mine down with the rest, it was fearful stuff burning like fire it took my breath from me and I could hardly raise my voice to Rosencranz for a cup of water which he supposed was what he handed me in the cup— It was after sun down when I opened my eyes again, and for some time could not divest myself of the idea that it was just morning and that I had not been to roll call or looked about the mess— I called out to know what time it was, and in an instant the tent was swarming with a crowd of my comrades some of them still very much intoxicated. I at once remembered the event of the morning and sang out for Rosencranz for an explanation which in his frank way, he soon did in this way— It was all a precunserted plan old fellow and I was but the instrument[. W]e wanted to have some fun out of you and thought getting you tight was the only way to do it, and only found out our mistake at our second dose to you, after which you fell over as if shot, and have been lying here ever since. Some of the boys wanted to carry the joke still farther but I would not allow it of course as your pard. I noticed a gloom amongst these still half intoxicated, which sat but ill on their countenance. I woke up from my twelve hours nap perfectly refreshed and felt half glad that I had thus escaped their present position. There had been in the regt especially in the Paducah company one of the most tremendous rows and free fights that had ever yet happened in it— Cob was under guard with several other, Capt. Solmes (our Capt) had been struck at the melley and it was hard to say who had not by the arms in slings and black eyes in the Company— I[t] appeared that after the first mornings dram, the devil got into everything, Cob and others made a rade on the Comisary and came back with buckets full [of] the hell fire. The row from this, one of the Company insulted Cob, who got a hatchet to make short work of him, other Companies we[re] brought in to quell the riot which had become by this time general as the whole Paducah company had ranged themselves on Cobs or his enemies side— The most sober joined the officers in quieting the rest, order was finally established—and all parties as they came to their proper senses, felt mortification and sorrow at the accurance, and my friends told me during the disturbance they had envied the quiet sleep I was enjoying. Their practical joke, I should have resented, especially on Rosencranz my little bed fellow, more strongly had it not been that I was thankful at heart that it had happened— Thus in the twilight I sat and wondered what they were doing in Rome, and whether a thought passed their minds of one far away from them, and who in thinking of them felt his unworthyness of any claim on them— A letter from home at this time would have been the greatest boon that could be granted me, but I was destined for many long months from that time to remain in ignorance of what they thought of my apparent neglect of family ties in leaving them so abruptly. Also the friends I had written to since I had joined the army seemed equally to have forgotten me, and it was not to be wondered at since I too had done the same on that day— Whiskey in a soldier's journal has often a part to play, for once that it may do him good and guard him against the cold and damp a hundred times it will crush in to the ground, or still worse make a beast of him in his own eyes as well as his friends— And yet a soldier and a canteen of whiskey, are always to be found in company. Temperance men and blue stockins may turn up their noses at men who do not think as they do, and the epicure of an evening sipping his ritch old wines, may do the same. But to a soldier who has felt the bitter cold wind at night, cutting through his tattered garments, and a wet blanket in the same state as the only covering between him and the pitiless storm will understand the comfort of a cup of anything no matter if it is warm from the distillery to purchase oblivion and sleep with—, and warm his empty stomach which had not had food for many a day— I should like to see these same sneering Pharisees if deprived of their luxuries, how they would like the preaching of a cold wet and empty stomach. Perhaps they would like a glass of water—, which they recommend—and seldom follow—

Many a time during my campaigning life has it been of immense service to me, and kept me from freezing on my post, and after battle when exhaustion would come on after the excitement of the fight, it would restore nature to its former equilibrium— I did not take it as medicine but that the effect was agreable more certainly than the infernal taste of the most of the stuff— Before driving whiskey from the rest of my journal, though even now I see where he may again intrude. I cannot but remember an incident in camp amongst the many connected with liquor which will show what artifice was resorted to by us to get it. An Irishman in Shephard Company, was known to a few of us, especially Bob Beard as the principal medium of importation[.] No one was allowed to enter camp except after going through an inspection by the sentinels as they entered. All the Whiskey shops in Bowlingreen had been closed and yet there was always plenty of the article in the old third, the Col and all the officers were on the qui vive to see where it came from, intending of course to put it to good use themselves— Pat had dodged them all first in one way and then another, one day he would have a coffee pot, with the spout stopped up with dowel and filled up with milk while the rest of the pot was full of prohibited beverage— When stopped by the sentinel he would poar a little of the milk out curse a little and pass on— He was found out at last and all eyes were on him even the Colonel was tempted from his ease to watch a favourable chance of getting a haul gratis— Pat kept up his usual suply for his customers to the wonderment of every body—

One morning early the Colonel caught sight of him coming up from the spring with two buckets, so suspicious was he that they might contain whiskey— That he sang out to him let me have a drink of your fresh water this bright morning. Pat scratched his head, gave him a knowing look and started towards the tent with one of his buckets, he had not gone half way, before the Col showed his hand by telling him that he wanted a drink out of the other bucket he had left behind— Says Pat they are both from the same spring whats the difference and with that gave a drink out of the second bucket, and the Col returned to his tent sold in finding it contained but water— None but a few of us knew that the sharp strategetic Irishman had outwitted the Col, and that the first bucket brought under the Col's nose, the principal ingredient of our evenings punch which we enjoyed all the more for the event—

When pay day came on, and we were mustered for that purpose, which was on the first of January 1861[, W]e got the first supply of money we had had for a long time— It was issued to us by the large sheet which we afterwards cut up for use, it looked strange to me for money, but money it was and we were soon parted with it— What did not remain in the hands of the skillful gamblers in the Co, was scattered in Bowlingreen by us in less than a week after the event— We had several dinners and general treats— One one occasion we had a squad sent in out of the company to arrest us, but they joined us in our fun and after ran down we were marched into camp as a working squad not having the countersign— by Sargt Turk— Ginger bread and lager bear were the luxuries of those days to us— I being with a party who it was my turn to treat, I went into a shop, where we were all served to bear and what [*January 1862*] ever we wanted by an Italian with whom I soon began to put my Italian to use, and who on my wishing to settle with him, refused to take anything from a Compatriotto,[68] which so much tickled the party I was with, that they wanted to hunt up a second one from the same country—

Our rations, especially our messes at this time were plentiful, with Bob Beard and the Chief Dick Turpin as providers— Guards were doubled on the Comisary things went worse than ever, George Harden and the rest of the Department would get in terrible rages and institute searches for the plunder but to no effect— One night it was my turn to guard the wagons, and although I would join the rest off duty in any attack they might make on the establishment, while on duty and trusted I felt bound to protect what I was placed their to guard— and when about midnight I heard somebody at the stores, I made a devil of a noise to let who ever it was get off, and came up at a charge bayonet, as the shadow from the wagon disappeared behind some tents— It might have been one of our mess for all I know This and the event of making the Lt Col mark time was the only incidents about camp guard duty that I remember— The latter gained me my reputation as a good sentinel— It happened thus. As I walked steadily and fast up and down my long and frozen beat to keep warm I saw a figure at the end of my beat, whom I first mistook for the next sentinel, but not seeing the glisten of his gun I sang out who come[s] there? the usual challenge— Friend with the Countersign was the answer. Which was instantly followed by the usual halt friend and give the countersign— and by this time I was up with the challenged party and my bayonet to his heart— I recognized at once our Lt Col Anderson, who reaching over my gun gave me what I knew to be the wrong Countersign— I told him he did not give me [the] right one, and had to remain there until the Coporal came— But said he you would not make me go back to the Col to get the countersign if the one I have given you is not the right one which I firmly believe you are mistaken about— and besides what can you do here I am right on your beat and saying so he sprang in the narrow path before me— I saw at once what he was up to, and brought my gun closer on to him, and without answering his question called Coporal of the guard Post No——. The Coporal was some time in coming, and the Col—told me I had done perfectly right and that I had the

68. A *compatriota* is a fellow countryman.

right to make him mark time until the Coporal came—and he began to mark time— When Coporal Lerch[69] came he tried to the same game on him but to no effect and going back to camp where he took him to he told him I had been the only sentinel who had stopped him and of course it coming from him it was a feather in my cap— Every body in camp heard it of course— Rome has made the Col mark time, bully for him etc. and when I got back to the guard tent I met a warm reception and we were all talking about— Many were about the guard tent who were not on duty but anxious to get the counter-sign to get out of the lines for a nights frolick—, when uncauscious-ly I let the cat out of the bag as the saying is—by falling in a second trap that was laid to find out the countersign for that purpose— I bet sayes one its some place in Mexico another was certain it was some state in the south, and I uncausciously said no Sacramento is in California, and thus all hands pounced on me and the tent and camp rang with laughter no longer at the Col but his Challenger— To describe the many instances of the transformation of Counter-sign in a night by the dutch and others on duty and the many mis-takes and blunders would take many a page to record— Andy [?], Rosencranz's substitute, invariably got the cart before the horse as in the case of Chapultepac and his metamorphises were amusing when they were not embarrassing— Grand rounds were then new things. One sentinel was much put out and remarked when they answered his challenge by grand rounds, Damit I thought it was the releif—Another more of a wag, as the releif was coming up, stum-bling over bushes and stumps sang out who comes there, the first man at the moment as he fell over one of the impediments in the road exclaimed "Jesus Christ" the other ordered him to halt and give the Countersign— On guard in the day time it was also amusing to see the ease, some would take on duty cleaning their guns—, play-ing cards or reading— One day Bob Beard and I were on guard next to each other, and as their was a grand parade for the Benefit of the Union men of Bowling to report to Buell,[70] every man was ordered

69. Probably John W. Leach. George, *History of the 3rd, 7th, 8th, and 12th Ken-tucky,* 167.

70. Don Carlos Buell (1818–1898) succeeded Sherman as commanding general of the Department of the Ohio in November 1861. When Grant moved on Forts Henry and Donelson in early 1862, Buell took Bowling Green. Boatner, *Civil War Dictionary,* 96–97.

out and the camp guard was forgotten for over six hours, but Bob and I did not. He got himself a chair out of the Cols Tent an one of his newspapers of which he gave me the full benefit of advertisements and all, while I seated on a stump made a sketch of him as a specimen of a Confederate soldier on duty— but that too has gone with all the rest of my sketches stolen at Louisville since the close of the war—

Our Col Tylman about this time was made Brigadier General and sent to Fort Henry — He bid his old regiment an affectionate farewell after an afternoon drill at which he complimented us highly on for the first time. We were sorry to loose him for although a strict disciplinarian and thought us no doubt what he said that a soldier was nothing but a stick, and treated them as such, yet we knew no one could lead us into battle better than him. He was thoroughly a military man in every respect and he gave his command— Soldem Hem— support hem, for the last time we were sorry it was so— He left us and his gallant conduct at the Post he was sent to increased our pride in him. Thompson was no military man, and but few liked him, Ben Anderson was the favorite and Capt Lyon famously [?] of the 3d Ky and then commanding a Battery was proposed as Lt Col— He gained the election amongst the soldiers. But some how or other Thompson became Col—Anderson Lt Col and Johnson[71] the segnor Capt Major— Soon after this Genl Buckner left us with the 2nd and 4th Ky and more than half of Johnsons force at Bowlingreen for Fort Donelson[72]— And the old staunch Commander presented a bold front to the Yankeys and kept his men [*February 1862*] always ready— We were marching as usual all the time to magnifie our numbers I suppose, build one set of Chilmneys to our tents, break up camp and build a new set— When the news came to prepare to march we were far in advance of our former quarters— near Bowlingreen, and as we marched down the turnpike near our old ground the lines of [illegible] now deserted looked as if there had been a tremendous army camp, where but a few thousand had changed camps— As we marched along in platoons to-

71. A. Johnson eventually rose to the rank of lieutenant colonel. George, *History of the 3rd, 7th, 8th, and 12th Kentucky,* 163.

72. Fort Henry fell on February 6, 1862; Fort Donelson was besieged by Union troops beginning on February 12 and surrendered on February 16. Boatner, *Civil War Dictionary,* 394–95.

wards Bowlingreen, I saw for the last Genl Albert Sidney Johnson, his gray hear and moustache was a shade grayer than when I had last seen him on parade, and a sad care worn look about his face as he stood in silence as we passed him sitting on his horse and surrounded by his staff. As we passed him, a flush of excitement rose on my face, as I looked at his gallant head and grand appearance, and felt pride in being commanded by such as him every man in the platoon as we moved by him seemed to step more firmly— We marched on past Bowlingreen and on towards Nashville, a shadow seemed to hang over us the same, which was to be seen on looking at Genl Johnson. After the first days march I was taken with a violent fever, I remember little after that, except of confused events— I must have been out of my senses at times— I found myself in an ambulance as we passed through Nashville and through the curtains of which I got a glimpse of the place large tall houses, women and children and old men on the streets in tears, at the sad sight of our leaving them to the Yankeys— Fort Henry and Fort Donelson had fallen the Yankeys wanted to cut us off and had Johnson retreated a day later they would have done so— When the army had reached the neighborhood of Nashville over the bridge of which the army had to pass in its retreat— the men were hastened on at a double quick to secure the exit— It seemed like a dream, the smoky barracks near Nashville, the Female seminary in Monfordsville[73] where were placed those on the sick list—from which I was sent on with a load of sick to Chatanooga— At Monfordsville, in looking around the room where I lay I saw a book which one of the soldiers gave, it was a young girls annual and her name was written in it, they had given up their place to the sick and the Yellow flag waved over it as over many a house in Nashville— When I was ready to leave and my friends had got me in an ambulance and given me several blankets which had been distributed promicuously at Nashville I felt sad indeed at the thought of being sent away from them—where to I knew not, and did not care much— I don't think any one could have felt more miserable than I did— Luckily I was not long in my senses—and remember nothing until I reached Chatanooga— I[t] was

73. The "female seminary at Munfordville" may have been Bethel College, a Baptist school for women in Russellville, about fifty to sixty miles from Munfordsville; or it could have been a co-educational school, the Green River Institute, in Hart County, which is about six to eight miles from Munfordsville.

late at night when we reached the station, at which we were turned out like a drove of swine, pell mell from the Box cars on to the Plat-[f]orm, the Surgeons counted us over, and I suppose made themselves comfortable— I felt badly and wrapped in my blankets I fell to sleep, in a baggage wheel barrow which was close at hand— When I woke up it was broad day-light and I found myself the only living object in [the] station, I felt already too miserable to feel the full force of my position— In a few minutes I came to the conclusion I had been overlook[ed] and left behind by the surgeons in charge, and so turned over and drew my hed under my blankets and was soon off again in dreamland— When I again woke, it was by a friendly nudge, and I opened my eyes to see a good natured kind face of a brother soldier, leaning over me with an enormous pie in his hand. I next noticed I was no longer in the part of the station where I first found myself— His words soon explained all. Well Partner, I hope you feel refreshed by your sleep, I never saw anyone sleep as hard, I rolled you out of the place I found to this which is better and have got a pie for you thinking you might be hungry when you woke up. I never shall forget that face it was a rough but benevolent one, and his interest in me showed his goodness of heart— I was hungry furiously so, for not a mouthful had I eaten for many a day. The pie gave me a desire for more food, and he helped me to get up and dragging my knapsack with my blankets I moved out of the station. I had not gone far before a gentleman going to his business I suppose came up and insisted in carrying my knapsack which weak as I was I would not allow him to do. In the principal street a sudden idea struck me to sell my watch which was the only property I had in the world— It was an old silver English one, and the [illegible] watchmakers the most they would give me was 15 dollars in Confederate money, badly in want that I was I would not part with my only treasure at such a price, and after much wandering of this kind weary and exhausted as night drew on I found my way into a carpenters shop and made my bed on his shavings— When they noticed me lying there, they did not say anything against it, and so at morning I thanked them and tried to find out from some soldiers about what I could do and to whom report— They asked if I would not like some soup to which I answered I would like very much so they took me to a place where pea soup was issued out by the cup full to invalide soldiers and beggars of all sorts— I eat more certainly then I ought to for my fever increased at night, and a surgeon took me in charge with a lot of sick bound for Atlanta Georgia— We left that evening on the train — and reached Atlanta the next night if I remember right— We remained in the street all night, as the hospitals were full, but in the morning we got bunks in an old Free Masons lodge which had been put to that use— It was frightful to behold the state of the place they called a hospital— The walls damp and stained and floor in a still worse state, no spittoons for the sick, a horrid smell, which the air coming through the broken windows could not dispel— What frightful scenes did I not witness in those walls— The cries of the dieing mingled with the card players oaths, the nurses and stuarts gambling while from my bed I could almost touch the three corpses who lay close to me untended from sunrise to sunset. The Doctor after feeling the pulses of his patients and precribing for them once and sometimes twice a day, washed his hands, put on his lavander colour kid gloves and adjusted his rose bud in his button hole, before dining out probably— All this I watched from my bunk, shivering with a chill, or with lips parched and dry and a burning forhead which but a little attention and cool water might have aleviated, but which I had no chance of getting—

Many a long day and night of suffering did I now pass— At first chills and fever, and then a most frightful fever when I was out of my head the most of the time and finally as I was thinking of once more seeing my old comrades in camps I was taken down with the measels, from which I only recovered with life, my constitution was completely ruined for ever, and I was but a ghost of myself— To recall now all the sufferings of the two months imprisement in different hospitals it would be both painful and useless— At times I thought I saw my family in Rome, and that I was completely forgotten, my letters were thrown in a corner unopened, and again— I would see my brother in the next regiment to me in the south, and the only recognition I met from [him] was the ordinary salute due from officer to private which he gave. In my madness it seemed that I had taken out my eyes and put them in a box for future use, and that my bed held me like a vice, and that I too was clamped on all sides. What moments of anguish were mine when recovering my senses. I glanced down the long corridor of the hospital on the living and the dead. One poor fellow died in the effort to resist the Dr who was trying to force him to take some liquor against his pledge to his mother that he never would. The Dr thought it necessary for his recovery, and the poor fellow, a youth hardly sixteen died with clenched teath, but true to the last breath to his promise to his mother. How imprudent in parents to thus sacrifice their children to an idea— Well do I remember an other poor fellow, wild with fever springing out of bed, cursing Drs and Nurses and swearing he would go to camps at once, and with his knapsack in his hand fell dead in the middle of the hospital floor but a few steps from his bunks— While things of this kind were of every day occurence, and I could not lift my hand to my forehead from weakness, an order came to remove all the patients that it was possible to the next hospital— I was taken up blankets and all with out being able to make any resistance, and carried through the cold streets to my new abode and put into a bunk near [a] window through whose windows the cold wind came with the snow— Luckily for me I had plenty of blankets, which the Paducah Co had given me and with my head under them lay and drempt of home and scenes of old. When I ventured to look out of a corner in the blankets, the same scenes I had witnessed in the first hospitals were again in view, only they were brought nearer home, by the fact of an old and well worn hat hanging at the post at the hed of my bed, while at my feet were the shoes iqually dilapidated of some poor fellow who had gone to the land where neither would be wanted. It was a shock to me to think I had been put right into the cold clammy bed of a dead man and my next thought was how soon might some one replace me in like manner. That night I did not sleep, the ghost of a former inmate of my bed seemed yet to hont it— The next night I begged to be removed from the neighborhood of the broken window panes, and the ghost which was always before me— This they did— Some ladies who had been sending provisions of all kinds to the sick, at last succeeded in getting into our den of filth and deprevation and found the sick with their coffee and corn dodgers for breakfast dinner and suppers and the Drs Stewarts and nurses, making use of the delicacies they had sent for us. There was one little lady who made her entry and declared she would see who got her basket of provisions this time. And to each she gave something. After this braking of the ice we fared much better— the ladies, who in a few days took charge of the establishment and cleaned it up, brought us any little delicacy they could think of. A cup of soup, or a glass of milk, were what we had never drempt of being able to taste again and they gave them to us— The convalescents had every thing they could wish for, eggnoag, cakes, pies, etc.— and some who could move about, I could see from my bunk go down one ile and come up an other, so as to meet the provisions both times and get double rations. One fellow who had something the matter with his head and ears, whenever any provisions were going around— would call out "Oh! my ear, Oh!—my ear, (I should so like to have a sweet potatoe) Oh my ear—" An other excentric fellow at the end of the hall, would always be calling out, Oh! man Oh! man, and died two days after I was there whith these two words on his lips—

Thanks to the kind hand that smoothed my pillow and soothed my fevered brain, and gave me healthy norishment, I began to re-cover my strength and was able to sit up in bed and sketch my friends in the adjoining bunks and our kind attendants. Miss Sally was amongst those who were most attentive to me, I was the only Vir-ginian in the hospital, and having made once a sketch of her and some ladies talking to the Drs I came to her notice. And one morn-ing waking up with a ravenous appetite such as follows a long ill-ness I was preparing to do justice to my mornings repast of coffee and corn dodger which still went the rounds when the ladies were not about. When low and behold what a suptious breakfast came in, I was wondering who the fortunate individual might be to enjoy it, when the old negroe woman with an enormous turband who had it— commenced calling out where is Miss Sallie's little Virginian and as I was pointed out as the fortunate one, in a moment I had all the eyes in the hospital turned on me. I felt as if I had committed some crime and for some time stared in wonder at the old negroe and her tray without thinking of what I was expected to do. I com-menced however on the wafels and soon finished the repast with a gusto and with many thanks to Miss Sallie— I turned over for a nap— That day I got a letter from Capt Somes enclosing me a little money that was coming to me, and telling me of an expected battle at Corinth. I determined to start at once before I was taken down by some new disease in this infectuous hole of a hospital. I managed to get up out of bed and get my traps together, no one seemed to care so that [they] got rid of me[.] I got my pass from the Dr and had a dinner downstairs with the Convalescents, and as we went down I had a glimpse of the Drs splendidly set out dinner, which was a great contrast to our light bread and boiled beef— I went into the kitchen and got a supply of this sort of food for the journey from the cook and with my bundle of blankets started for the depoes, got my transportation to Corinth— And as I had a few hours left I sauntered about town, I had about twenty dollars, which I invested in a paint box, having for some time hesitated whether to have my teeth filled or get the box, and concluded that the gold I already had in my teeth might be picked out by some Yankey on a battlefield yet— I was going down the principal street when two pretty girls rushed out of a soldiers home establishment, calling out ["T]here goes our little soldier, come back my little man and let us see what you have got in your haversack." Of course I obeyed at once, and a look into my dirty only half filled haversack soon disgusted them, and they tossed it into the air and gave me a fresh one, and filled it full of provisions of all kind, dried beef cakes and I know not what all and a bottle of Black berry wine besides[.] I felt like kissing them but contented [*March 1862*] myself with blessing them in my heart and, as we parted—one of them was my pretty little hospital friend, whose kindness I shall always remember and who I hope yet to meet again and be able to express my gratitude to—

When I reached Corinth every body had gone to the front. It was Sunday morning— The battle had commenced courriers were going to and from Corinth. After a meal on hard tack and brown sugar out of the barrel at the depot— The Party of us bound for the battlefield managed to get on top of some wagons which were sent on for the wounded. As we approached the battle ground the sound of musketry and artillery which seemed to become more and more distant at each moment, told that our troops were advancing on the enemy— Nearer and nearer we got to the scene of the action[.]

We left the wagon and trudged along as fast as we could toward the field of action[. I]t was however getting late in the day, and the sun was but three or four hours high. Negroes were hurrying to the rear with the spoils of the dead. One of the party sang out, Hellow Sam! have you seen the elephant. Lor bless you Massa, we just seen the tip of his tail and dat nearly scare the wits out of us and away they went. On we pushed and soon met some wounded that were being carried to the rear. It was through them we got the first tidings of our glorious victory. My first inquiry was about the 3d Kentucky and was told that there was nothing left of them, and as to the Paducah Co—there not a single member left. But I soon after saw

Keon who gave me all the news. The Regiment what remained of it was close by and the days fighting over. The old third although belonging to the reserve under Breckinridge has been called into action in the early part of the day, and had suffered sevearly from a ambush, but the reports I had heard were very much exagerated. Keon had a riffle he had got from a Yankey, and the other members of the company, a gay plumed hat of some commander of the same tribe— they were in good spirits although the wounded and dieing were all around us, and gave glorious news of the days work. Rosencranz had covered himself with glory leading a charge— and although the list of wounded and dead was a long one, no one could resist the triumph of the moment. No one but a soldier can understand the bitter disappointment and mortification of being too late, and looking on his comrades who have each one his story of adventure to recount, and in a crowd like this a new arrival with an unfired gun makes a sorry figure. The surgeons were at work lopping off limbs and binding up others- there part of the battle had arrived, and the agonizing cries that came from their tents told but too clearly what was going on in there. The rows of poor fellows who had fallen under the knife or saw of these I fear many of them but little skilled proffessioners, were stretched out before the tent, and every now and then an other was placed on the roll of the next world. One, poor fellow, as they were [*April 1862*] tugging his arm away, cooly asked the Dr to remove his sweethearts ring from the finger of his dismembered hand. Others would not take a drop of Cloreform, and died under the knife with a smile on their lips. Others yelled like fun, and the Drs. always said they were hurt the least and would get well. Poor Gid Garret. The boys just before going into the fight told him, if the Yanks hit him at all, they wished it would be in the mouth for he was the most inveterate talker in the regt and sure enough a bullet passed from jaw to jaw without any great injure than making two wholes in his skin and knoking out three or four teath. He had his mouth open at the time. Poor Husband[74] was in a bad way and many others who had been left on the field. As we were talking all together, and the wounded joining in the fun Gid Garret would give a most ridiculous smile, and look what he would have given worlds to be able to say. The sun was setting I remember it well, when the voices of regiments coming in from the field, called our attention to the road, the glisten of the bayonets soon were followed by the unmistakable gray, which was visible here there through their Yankey overcoats, others Yankey cheeses on their bayonets, hams, womens clothes, and traps of all kinds out of the Yankey camps, and merrily they sauntered by each one with his share of the plunder and almost every man with a gun besides his own and some as many as three or four— That night as we sat around the camp fires and talked the battle over, many a poor fellows sreak went up from the field where it was fought, as the artillery changed position in the dark and could not avoid going over some of them— The Texas rangers[75] were at the front with the cavalry and many a regiment camped on Yankey tents and eat their supper, as the[y] did their breakfast in the morning. A group of Texas rangers were having a social game of poker for some Yanky spoils on a body of a Yank and in his mouth they had stuck a chunk of lighted pine wood— so I was told. To recite half I was told on that memorable night would take a long time to write, and I shall confine myself to what I saw— and underwent myself. I slept soundly from my long tramp, and disgust at being too late, and early in the morning I was sturing helping the poor fellows that were hurt. After breakfast a party headed by George Haiden proposed to visit the battle field and help the wounded there and burry the dead. We were formed into a detail all of us with white tape around our arms as badges of our office, and I with my pencil and book to make a sketch. We had not got far when, drums began to beat to arms, and a great commotion commenced on all sides, it was fall in here, where is my regiment I want to get with it. Never mind fall in here any where, and officers were forming their men on all sides. I took off my white badge, and was not long in equipping myself from a dead Yankey whom it seemed that providence had dropped close to me to help me out. I was delighted to find his gun in order, and his cartridge box well filled. Perhaps it was with the poisoned bulets they had been shooting at us the day before.[76] A squad was forming close by and I fell in with them, a

74. H. L. Husband. George, *History of the 3rd, 7th, 8th, and 12th Kentucky*, 167.

75. Col. John A. Wharton's Texas Regiment Cavalry. James Lee McDonough, *Shiloh—In Hell before Night* (Knoxville: Univ. of Tennessee Press, 1977), 247.

76. On Sunday, April 13, 1862, the *Memphis Daily Appeal* reported that "packages of poisoned balls were found on the field [at Shiloh]—also poisoned quinine, which the enemy allowed to be smuggled across the lines." Chapman's memory of this alleged war crime may have been based on this article or on the rumors that inspired it.

black whiskered Louisiana officer[77] was in command of this little troop half of which had never seen each other before. We stood up together and knew we were fighting as one man— We soon faced to the right and were marched off to join others formed in the same way— We were got into a line on a hill close by and a Louisiana colonel with his arm in a sling took command of this battalion which was larger by this time than any brigade on the field. We were exposed very much where we were and the shells commenced to come rather thick when we were removed to [a] ravine below— It was here that I first saw general Beauregard[78] and an imposing sight it was to see him riding quietly along with his staff all in bright coloured shirts which seemed as a mark for the enemy. A hearty cheer came up from our line, and soldiers stopped from eating Yankey cheese and oysters which were passed allong the line to give him a hearty cheer— We were told to cheer, and cheer again, and fresh fuwel was added to our excitement and cheers by the report which were evidently spread we found out afterwards for that purpose that

77. The officer Chapman speaks of was probably Lt. Col. Charles Jones of the 17th Louisiana, who was wounded in the left arm on the first day. In his report of April 11, Jones told how he sent his adjutant to form the regiment "near the Big Spring" on the morning of the April 7. The "Big Spring" may have been Water Oaks Pond, a wet-weather pond located about a quarter-mile north of the intersection of the present Federal and Confederate Roads; it was near this pond that the Confederates made their counterattack on the second day. Jones continues: "I with what few men I had, managed to gather together about 200 in all, composed of stragglers ordered by General [Daniel] Ruggles to advance. The general at this instance rode in front of the lines and, seizing the flag from the hands of the color-bearer, gallantly led them to the charge." *The War of the Rebellion: A Compilation of the Official Records of the Union and Confederate Armies*, 128 vols. (Washington, D.C.: Government Printing Office, 1880–1901), ser. 1, vol. 10, 1:506–7. Ruggle's report (pp. 470–74) lacks the necessary details to trace his movements that day.

78. Beauregard could well have led this counterattack. According to Roman, "At about one o'clock P.M. [on April 7] the enemy, on our left, being reinforced, had resumed the offensive. General Bragg . . . was gradually driven back, towards the Shiloh meetinghouse. He then sent to General Beauregard for assistance. Fortunately, in the small ravine passing immediately south of the meetinghouse were the 18th Louisiana and the Orleans Guard battalion, together with two Tennessee regiments, which had been collected there in obedience to orders. General Beauregard rode down to them, addressed a few words of encouragement to the first two, and ordered them to move promptly to the support of General Bragg. As they passed by, with a tired, heavy gait, they endeavored to cheer their own favorite commander, but

Price Van Dorne and even Jeff Davis himself were on the field[79]—
Hearty cheer after cheer resounded from all sides, those who knew
our cheer took courage and we our selves were deceived— The Yankeys had however from the previous days work learned to fear that
sound—

As soon as our hurried repast was finished we were again put
into motion, to the front and when the charge was made forward,
Hardee[80] himself rode to the front and with his battle flag in his
hand led us on— I turned to [a] near man, and asked him what regiment he belonged to[. I]t was the ———, and asked him if I was
wounded to help me and receive the assurance that I would do likewise for him if he needed it, and thus as we moved on pressed hands
with him as a seal of our compact. There was not a soul near whom
I had ever known before— We advanced over broken and tangled
ground trees had been cut down across our path both by the axx and
cannon—My hat was caught by a twig as we moved on, but it was
no time to look back on —on and on we moved keeping our line as
best we could. Double quick boys, we will soon be on them, and a
few fellows fell in our rear as we advanced and saw the blue coats of
the enemy looming in the distance— Our officer cautioned us to
aim low and take deliberate aim— We came to a halt where we had
good cover— and soon the blue bellys commenced to show themselves more clearly— and the order was given to commence firing—
Bang bang and the work commenced— I had little time to look about

---

were so hoarse from fatigue and overexertion that they could only utter a husky
sound, which grated painfully on General Beauregard's ear.... [Then] he rode with
his staff, to the leading regiment of Pond's brigade, the 18th Louisiana ... and seizing
its colors, ordered his 'Louisianans' to follow him." Alfred Roman, *The Military Op-
erations of General Beauregard in the War Between the States, 1861 to 1865*, vol.1 (New
York, 1884), 317.

79. Maj. Gen. Sterling Price and Maj. Gen. Earl Van Dorn were in Arkansas at
the time. Van Dorn's army, which had been defeated at Pea Ridge in March, was not
to join Beauregard until after the battle. As Johnston's reputation plummeted after
the evacuation of Nashville, Beauregard had urged President Jefferson Davis to take
command of the army in the West. See McDonough, *Shiloh*, 60, 69.

80. Chapman remembered the general who led the charge as Hardee, but while
Hardee did personally lead numerous charges on the second day, he was in action on
the far right of the Confederate line, not in Conrad's part of the battlefield. See
Nathaniel C. Hughes, Jr., *General William J. Hardee: Old Reliable* (Baton Rouge: Louisiana State University Press, 1965), 110.

but there were gallant things done on all sides, fellows braving the whole thing, [m]any going in front of the line placing a tree between them and the main line— But it was load and shoot all the time, fellows fell on all sides of me and a thought crossed my mind that the hand of death might be hovering close to me at the time— For a soldier to describe a battle, it is impossible to do so for he never sees but the incidents immediately near him and even those through a mist as it were of powder and excitement. I remember the Colonel with his wounded arm pointing to the front, the cartridges beginning to give out of my box, and the feeling that I was about to fire my last when, suddenly as I was ramming it down, I felt as if a hot cannon ball had struck me on the head, and remember nothing more as I must have fainted that very moment from loss of blood. When I came to I found my gun gone and the fellows around me saying it was no use taking him off the field he has gone up at the spout[81]— Look at his head— I had not the courage to open my eyes, my first movement was to feel if I still lived— if such a sensation can be understood. The terrible feeling of that moment I shall never forget— Every action of my life seemed written before me— When I opened my eyes the battle was still going on, and many had bit the dust like myself— I put my hand to my head where I remember having been struck for I felt no pain— and my hand when I looked at it told a fearful story and I felt the warm blood running down my back in a perfect stream— I looked for the man I had called on to help me before the battle, but he was near a tree and perhaps wounded also for when I beckoned to him he took no notice, so I had to crawl as best I could to a tree close by, after having made several vain efforts to rise. I put the tree between me and the foe for the battle still raged all around. While drooping in this way my head leaning against the tree, I noticed a little violet looking up to me from under the trampled grass, and a thought of past scenes of a different nature passed through my mind as I plucked it and put it in my sketchbook next to my bosom. It is strange how one little thing in Gods creation can turn ones mind from scenes such as I was then surrounded by— That little flower I carefully kept and pressed in my journal as the only trophy I took from the fire of battle—

81. To have "gone up at the spout" meant to be in a bad way—in this case, being mortally wounded. Partridge, *Dictionary of Slang*, 815.

I could feel that my wound had been made by a musket ball, but whether the intruder was in their or not of course [I] could not be sure off, although I supposed it must have made its exit otherwise I would not have my thoughts about me. I began to feel more and more faint, and should have dropped over, but for one of the ambulance corps of the third who recognized me and took me to an ambulance and thence to the Drs Tent. When old Dr Thompson[82] looked into my wound for a moment, his usual gruff joking tone changed, and he told me in a soft kind voice, which scared me, that it looked bad, and that I would have to get out and he would see what he could do for me, but that it was no use to do anything then, but as I could not get on, I had better lay quietly in his tent, and if the Yankees came up I would be taken care of all the same. I got out and the ambulance went back for more wounded—The Dr gallopped off to meet an other ambulance coming up and I remained with my wound still bleeding at [a] tremendous rate by a tree— Reports came in that our troops were still holding the position but it was not certain how long they would be able to— A little wiery unhurt man was near me and offered to help me along so with a stick to lean on and his shoulder I managed to get on, one fellow I passed through me his handkerchief another his hat and thus with my wound doubly covered I did not feel the cool breeze playing with it and my hear— My little friend had a supply of Yankey candy he had got which he gave me to eat, and I could not help smiling at his kindness and forethought for the journey, which promised to be a slow one for me at least. We stopped by a running brook and an old negroe lent me his tin cup to bathe my wound—and drink— further on we were abruptly stopped by a cavalry man, who dashed up at such a rate that he knocked off my hat, but as soon as he did it apologized, and turned to my companion to know if he was hurt. Otherwise he had orders that none should pass. The little fellow whined out I am looking out after my poor friend and thus passed through the line of guards to prevent just his tribe of stragglers from getting away. However he got me this far, and if he had not done intirely his duty through the day I felt thankful to him for what he had done for me. I stopped to rest however a few moments afterwards and he stepped

82. J. W. Thompson, surgeon. George, *History of the 3rd, 7th, 8th, and 12th Kentucky,* 163.

aside and never returned. I regretted it the more as he was my comisary— I managed as best I could from tree to tree and stump to stump, accasionally making an appeal to a wagon going by but to no effect as they were loaded down with men that could not walk, some of them as they jostled along over the rough road in springless wagons gave most pitiful groans, which made me forget that I too was hurt. As night drew on I managed to get into a house near by, the floor of which was covered with wounded— What a quaint little house it was, and the inmates of it were quite in keeps, one woman was nursing a young fellow on the only bed in the place. He seemed a great friend of Genl Poke's who wished to cheer him up and in fact all of us, by recounting the looks of the battle field after the fight. Our troops were still in possession, and there were at least three blue coats stretched out for one gray. Every body was talking at the way Cob's battery laid them low on sunday— It was here I first learned of the death of our noble Commander Genl Albert Sidney Johnson— And the victory of the two days battle seemed won at a frightful sacrifice—[83]

Next morning by day brake I was on the move again toward Corinth. My wound pained me a little for the first time and I wet it several times during the days march. A rain came on towards evening, as I trudged along the muddy road— Several times I tried to get a lift, but with no success, and towards night, I spred my blanket under a wagon, having had the first food since the previous day, a few wet crackers I found in an old barrel along the road, a provision of which I put in my haversack for the following day— I forget whether it was two or three days after this that I reached the old third again or not. I remember I was completely played out as they say, several miles from Corinth and had given up going any further for the day, when a Cavalry man came along and offered me a place behind him on his horse, which I gladly accepted and in a few hours was once more amongst old comrades of the Paducah Co from whom I met a hearty welcome—In the pleasure of seeing them, many of whom were badly wounded I forgot my own hurt, until someone remarked [on] my bloody handkerchief, and a Dr took me in charge,—

83. Chapman was probably referring to Maj. Gen. Leonidas Polk, the Confederate commander who fought at Shiloh. Lt. Robert Cobb's battery suffered heavy losses. See Davis, *The Orphan Brigade*, 90.

I was laid out in a log house and after a good washing and the hair cut out of the place, my wound was dressed for the first time. The Dr thought as did all my other friends that I had made a narrow escape, as my scull in one place was not thicker than an eggshell, and the ball had made a course of nearly a half circle around my head, but luckily had some respect for my feelings[84]— I felt so much refreshed after and a good grubb the first I had had since the battle that I was very much astonished when I found I had to start that evening for Memphis with a crowd of other wounded. I protested to Capt Solmnes, for independent of feeling very well in every respect— I did not fancy the idea of going back to a hospital— It was no use, they told me they had no use for disabled men and so I had to. It was lucky that I did, for had I not been well attended to I have but little doubt, from events that followed I would not have lasted but a few weeks. A twiching pain would shoot through me occassionally, and although at the time I thought it nothing, I soon found that a wound was not as easy a thing to get over as I thought.

We were all packed into box cars and started off at last toward grand junction. Husbands and Johnny[85] and others were in the same car with me.

On the road about ten or fifteen miles from Grand Junction the cars ran or rather jumped off the tract. In a few seconds it was all over. At first it seemed as if we were jostling over rocks and then suddenly found ourselves jumbled in a heap in the corner of the car

84. Dr. John D. Reid, M.D., a pathologist, has examined this account and believes that "the fact of Chapman's survival, large wound, and a lack of an exit argue for a spent ball (or in this case with trees, more likely a ricochet)." Dr. Reid has also written that "the statement that the ball had made a course of nearly a half circle around his head implies that it was known where the bullet was; in the absence of x-rays, this further implies that it could be felt and was beneath the scalp. Had it entered, say, near the hairline in front and passed backwards it could have lodged close to the mid line in the occipital region;the galea aponeurotica is quite thick and it is conceivable that it actually curved slightly before coming to a full stop." Letter to the author, September 8, 1986. The bullet that struck Chapman probably made a long tunnel-like passage called at that time by the French term *plaies en seton*. In such cases, a counteropening was made to extract the ball and the wound was washed by injections to remove foreign materials. The later "probing" of his wound in the Overton Hospital was probably an attempt to drain it and/or apply medication. See Joseph K. Barnes, ed., *The Medical and Surgical History of the War of the Rebellion*, vol. 2 (Washington, D.C.: Government Printing Office, 1875), 94–95, 119–20.

85. Probably John Rochelle.

which was smashed in several places by the fall. We scrambled out as best we could from the bottom and the side and found the whole train in a perfect wreck, our car had made the highest and the furthest leap, and had taken the telegraph with it as it went over the embankment. It happened as I remember right in this way. The tender was an old one, and the back wheels got loose and came off impeding the progress of the engine, and knocking us for the first off the track and we dragging the rest after us. It was a tremendous smash up and the corpses laid stretched all along the road. Our car was the only one that escaped without some one killed. It was frightful to see, so many with their arms in slings and bandaged legs stretched out in this way. All on the train were wounded and the shock was terrible on them. I shall never forget the jumble of wretches screaming and cursing in our car, as we were tossed up in a heap. The surgeons were at their work again and some were saved but many a brave fellow ended his days at this spot. All the people in the immediate neighborhood came with or sent us releif, and in a few hours a new train came for us from Grand Junction and we got in safe. The people here were all anxious to serve us in some way. Pretty young ladies with bandages and lint for the most needy. Old ladies with knit socks, little girls with flowers and cakes. Negroes men and women with more substantial food for those that might feel like a snack, and for about two hours we were entertained in this sumptious style. To say we enjoyed it would be saying too little. We gloried in [the] spirit of the people and blessed them from the bottom of our hearts. Parsons with tracts for the soldier so— After sharing their hospitality and taking a short rest we moved on again by rail, and reached Memphis at night.[86]

A crowd of friends were at the station to meet us, and learn the news of the great battle, and of their friends. Many was the sad story we had to tell them of lost or wounded comrades, and the tears of the widowed and orphaned made us forget our own suffering. Several who had come on with us were claimed at once by relatives and friends and those that were not were distributed around at the different hospitals. Husbands and myself were taken to the Over-

86. On Friday, April 11, the *Memphis Daily Appeal* reported: "RAILROAD ACCIDENT A serious accident occurred to a train on the Charleston railroad yesterday about four miles east of Grand Junction. By the displacement of a pair of trucks, several cars were thrown from the track suddenly, while the train was moving with speed."

ton Hotel[87] which had been turned into a hospital. It was a splendid building and had only a short time been finished, the marble steps and ritch tapestry contrasted strangely in the dazzling gas light with gastly faces and tattered clothes. We found beds— real beds, imagine our astonishment, prepared for us and after a warm plait of soupe, I fel asleep— I drempt of past times, and faces that I had not seen for years—. It seemed I was no longer a soldier, but once more in the happy land of the past, I felt a gentle touch on my sholder, and the illusion was increased, when on opening my eyes, I beheld two lovely girls, leaning over me, and their curls touching my cheek, what I saw I know not, but they smiled and told me they had to disturb me to dress my wound. All flashed back on me in an instant where I was and I thanked God I had fallen in such hands. They smoothed my pillow, and looked a blessing on me and I slept on until late the next day— When I was awoke by Casy our fifer,[88] entertaining a whole crowds of Ebony imps with his old phife. He was playing Dixie and I again thought I was in camp, so strange did every thing seem to me. Casy was one of the Phifers, in fact the last of the Phifers, of the old third— In the battle he had put his Phife in his pocket and sholdered a gun and had done good service with the rest of us, and had limped off the battle field with a fractured leg and half a dozen . . . fifes of all shapes and sizes—which he was trieing to swop off with negroes for whiskey— During the day he gave us several of his lively tunes as he called them, which were anything but entertaining. He was propped up in bed with his leg all bandaged up a picture for punch blowing on his infernal phife— A Yankey above us who dieing sent down word if he would play Yankee Doodle, which he did of course. The only use his phife was to us, was in bringing the negroe waiters about, and our room was the best attended in the Hospital I believe. Each day some one would come in and claim some of the wounded and in a short time there was but one besides myself in the room. My wound was a great attraction to a lot of little medical students, and they used to come in and discuss

87. The Overton Hotel had been converted to a military hospital after the Battle of Belmont, Missouri, on November 7, 1861. It was equipped with an operating room, surgeons' offices, and a pharmacy. Patricia M. LaPointe, "Military Hospitals in Memphis, 1861–1865," *Tennessee Historical Quarterly* 42 (Winter 1983): 327.

88. T. F. Casey, musician. George, *History of the 3rd, 7th, 8th, and 12th Kentucky,* 165.

over it and probe it until my very blood curdled at their sight and would not let any one meddle with it except the regular Dr.[89] The two young ladies that took me in charge the first night I got there, would come occasionally to see how we were getting on until the Dr stopped it, and then ever[y] corner over design in the papering was studied out. I longed for a change in some way, my wound was paining me and the Drs had so much to do that a whol day would pass without its being dressed. One day I was not feeling bright by any means and my bed began to be earksome- and no sight of a friendly face was near to cheer the dreary hours that hung so heavily on me. No books, not a word from any body. I wished again for the tiresome phipher, but he too had met friends to care for him, or perhaps his broken leg had carried him on the voyage so many comrades were every day traveling. I was told that Husbands (who I had not seen since we entered the hospital together) and myself were to leave in charge of George Haiden for a Mrs. Browns[90] of Ky, where we were to remain until we had recovered from our wounds— Husbands was stout and healthy looking and his wound not being visible to all eyes as mine, this added to my having been ill before the battle, when we reached Mrs. Browns they thought that I was nearer deaths door than poor Husbands— We were put in the same room and that dear kind lady for whom I shall ever preserve the warmest recollection and friendship nursed us as if we had been her own brothers. No greater care could have been taken of us anywhere. . . . Mrs. Brown or her sister Miss Horde[91] would come up and dress our wounds three times the day, and their friendly physician attended to us— Husbands had been consigned from the hospital as a flesh wound, and the Dr administered treatment accordingly wet bandages etc.— as was done towards me. The second day we were together he com-

89. There were two medical colleges in the city, the Memphis Medical College and the Botanico Medical College, both founded in 1847. Because instruction at these institutions was suspended at the beginning of the war, the "lot of little medical students" were probably medical cadets or former students from one or both of the two schools. Patricia LaPointe to the author, Mar. 13, 1987. See also Ms. LaPointe's book, *From Saddlebags to Science: A Century of Health Care in Memphis, 1830–1930* (Memphis: Health Sciences Museum Foundation, 1984), 52–53.

90. Mrs. Sarah Brown's boarding house was located on Madison between Third and Fourth Streets. *William's Memphis Directory City Guide and Business Mirror* (Memphis: Cleaves and Vaden, 1860), 99.

91. Mrs. Hordly boarded at Mrs. Brown's. *William's Memphis Directory*, 198.

plained less—and had been reading to me all day—, and as night drew on and they sent us up our tea, I went to his bed to give him his, when he tried to open his mouth to swallow it and, felt a difficulty in speaking even, but told me that he could not and that his jaws seemed to be closing—Lock Jaw. My God, was my first thought, I rang the bell as hard as I could, and all rushed up from the supper table to see what it was and poor Husbands was getting worse and worse, and his jaws gradually closing, the Dr was sent for and as soon as he saw him pronounced that there was no hope—

[*Facing page:* It was frightful to see death stealing on him gradually and clenching{?} with an {illegible} his jaws until a gurgling sound and a nervous twitch through his frame told that his work was done, the mustles relaxed and his features from the distortion of pain settled to a composed and quiet expression, and when we closed his eyes he looked like one only asleep—]

Poor fellow, what agonies he endured all night—at day brake he was a corpse with as lovely a smile on his face as I ever saw— He was but eighteen poor fellow, and to think he might have been saved, if amputation had been used in time, both bones of his leg were shattered and you could twist [them] any way you liked, and yet he had been operated upon and pieces of the bone extracted and yet he was left in this state. If it was not murder it looked very like it from the hands of the surgeons— In the morning he was dressed for the last roll, and as he lie on the bed awaiting his coffin, he looked so much at peace and pleasing that I took out my pencil and made a sketch of him as he lie, thinking of his mother all the time, and that if it may be a comfort to her to have some remembrance of him no matter how insignificant. I was suddenly startled by a voice close to me, a little darkeys, who asked me in the most composed way possible, who would make my picture when I was dead— This simple remark brought up a new train of ideas which were not much brighter than the previous ones. Poor Husbands, what a tigress you had for a mother, no not a tigress for she loves her young, but what a depraved creature she must have been to have uttered the remark she did when the news of her sons death reached her— "I had two sons in the rebel army they were both scoundrels and I am thankful they are both dead—" Was it for this unnatural woman I was making his drawing. I left it with Mrs. Brown, when I heard his mothers remark— I was prevented from my wound from seeing him to his last resting place. The recollection of that frightful night often haunted me in the quiet of my sick room— If it were possible the kindness of Mrs Brown and her household seemed to increase from that day towards me and every imaginable care was taken of me—

At last I was alowed to go down and be with the family. How delightful it was to sit on their back porch those bright spring morning, everything cheerful and bright, my kind nurses with their needlework, and the children playing with the little negroe in the sunlight. . . . My pencil would often come into requisition at these times and the lines I traced which would have brought back those pleasant scenes again are no longer where I can look at them—but the recollection will always remain. These kind people knew nothing of me and I was nothing to them but a soldier in the Paducah Co—from which little town they came from and yet how they petted and spoiled me— Fancy a rough soldier living in Luxury as I was after the life I had led in camp— They would often ask me to tell them about Rome, and I retraced old times of my home there with a pleasure in which I seemed to live them over again— What projects I formed for after the war, when I could show my appreciation of there kindness in some way— Time has passed since then, many a year and I have never seen or heard of them except when Mrs. B— sent my journal and sketches which I left with her to a friend of fathers in Louisville and where they were stolen or lost— How faithfully were they kept through all the troubles in the south by this kind lady up to [the] end of the war and I unfortunately sent for them—

One evening while enjoying the afternoon cool breeze on the front of the portico, some people living opposite who had just found out who I was, and that I was some relative of theirs by my mother, invited me over to see them—I remember how Mrs. Brown wanted me to wair Mr B—— close on the occasion, but I stuck to my old gray and only tried them on to please her. How strange I looked and felt in them. I remember the visit was may [made?], they wanted to do anything and everything for me but there it ended—

Major King from Paducah staid at the Browns for some time— and Bill Milligan[92] also for a while—I sketched them both in fact

92. Probably Capt. George A. King, a company commander in the 5th Kentucky Regiment, who was wounded at Shiloh. *Memphis Daily Appeal*, Apr. 18, 1862. "Milligan" was William Milliken of Company D, 3d Kentucky Regiment. George, *History of the 3rd, 7th, 8th, and 12th Kentucky*, 167.

every one that came in my way. My mornings were passed painting a little picture of Mrs. Browns two little children— The baby was patient enough not knowing any better, but the pretty little girl with golden ri[n]glets, her bright blue eyes used often to flash fire, as she would wish the "Yankees to cut off my head" next time so that I could not paint her again which I often threatened to do. Miss Horde I also made a sketch of, which she was much pleased with, as I succeeded in flattering her a little, which is always agreeable to the fair sex— Capt. Sohnes was in Memphis for a short time, and we went to the theater together— One night Genl Jeff Thompson Indian orderly was there while a performance was going on of some Indian war dance, and could not resist the impulse to give a loud shout, at which the whole theater was startled, and the performance seaced for a few moments. The most of the audience were in their shirt sleeves and some with but little on their backs, being of Prices bare-footed command, and yet the[y] cheerfully cracked their jokes and peanuts and chucked the shells at the actors. While at Memphis they were [*May 1862*] asked which they would have tents or whiskey and to a man they voted for the latter.[93]

Capt. Sohnes insisted I was not fit to return to camp, but as I found out what he was up to, for an other fight was hourly expected at Corinth[.] I packed up my duds, and got ready to start— Having had the experience of one battle already I knew better how to prepare for a second. And so I wrote a long letter to my mother and sealed it with my journal and sketches which I left with Mr Brown to be sent to Rome if I should never return to claim it—and they heard positively of my death. Having done this I felt much more at ease, although I always was more or less oppressed with anxiety about my home and family, as not a line had reached me since I left there— I wrote however as usual by every opportunity I could get hoping that some of my many letters might reach them— At times I thought that my action in leaving as I did had condemned me in their light for ever which I could not feel that I intirely deserved— I

93. Brig. Gen. M. Jeff Thompson of the Missouri State Guard, was a flamboyant partisan fighter along the Mississippi River. The odd reference to him as "Indian orderly" may be Chapman's confusion of the officer with Indian fighters recruited by the Confederacy in Arkansas and Missouri. "Price" was Maj. Gen. Sterling Price. For both Thompson and Price, see Jay Monaghan, *Civil War on the Western Border, 1854–1865* (Boston: Little, Brown, 1955).

often wondered also why all my other friends to whom I had written had likewise neglected me— What Had I done that all the world was against me—

In the midst of these sad reflections Mrs Brown came up to my room to bid Milligan and me good bye, as we left in the morning, and the farewell of that kind and affectionate lady made me forget my [isolated?] position—

We were soon back in camp again with the Old Third at Corinth. My wound still held on and had not healed up intirely, so that I still wore my head bandaged up— All the boys crowded to see two comrades just from town and enjoy what we had brought them. I thought myself quite a guy, while in Memphis in my gray jacket which had only a little brushing up and mending and a little blacking to my boots and a clean collar occasionally, and yet these had made such a transformation in me, that my comrades threatened to turn me out of the mess if I did not go back to old "Rome" as I used to be— All my collars I know went all the same the first Sunday in camp, and I had to give up town habits sure enough—

Boys who does not remember camp life at Corinth—what water we had to drink and how we had to watch the little we got at night as it used to rise out of the clayish oily ground into the shallow pits we dug for fear of others stealing it—and the Jews coming down by the train with water to sell fancy a dime a drink— Many was the curse we put on this race as we indulged in the luxury of one good drink before dining— May they need the water they sold us to quench the flames of Hell burning their infernal carcasses— Wherever you go you find a Jew exacting his pound of flesh— In the swamp of Louisiana, in the little village on the battlefield (after the fight) where in the south did you not meet them except in the army where they ought to have been made to go—

One day while in the miserable town of Corinth—buying some pickles and things from the Jews I saw a face I thought I recognized and clapped Dr Captdevielle on the back my old friend who had crossed on the City of Manchester with me I had not seen him before since we parted near Hopkinsville in Ky.[94] He was glad to see

94. Auguste Capdeville, whom Conrad had met on his voyage to America in 1861, served as one of the three surgeons of the Orleans Battery, which saw action at Shiloh (where the corps lost a third of its number) and at Corinth. It was orga-

me and we went around to the hospital together, he belonged to the Orleans Guards battery and introduced me as his son to a very charming person from N.O who was there and seemed to be a great friend of his. We afterward went to his camp, which was like a French colony, everybody speaking French and looking French. Plenty of sigarettes and wine and delicacies of all kinds. The creoles were well uniformed and had more of the appearance of what in Europe they would call soldiers, but none of the determined weather beaten, hardened look our Ky. boys had. These Creoles looked as if they would fight and indeed they did splendidly at Shiloh—but not as if they would indure the sufferings we already had with a groan— They had been away but a few weeks from the Cresent city and yet they already longed to be back in spight of the Yanks being there. When I left them I felt satisfied they would not hold on with us long and they did not. Capdeveille returned with them and I never heard of him again. Beauregard gave them the devil in one of his speaches— Although he was a Creole himself—

On or about the 7th of May 1862 I arrived at Corinth from Memphis my wound from Shiloh had nearly healed up intirely, and it was with delight I greated the sight of the green trees and fields once more. I believed I would soon be perfectly well again, but what a sad mistake I was under. My health was not good when I got there, and the retched water from the muddy wells in our camps soon did the work for me and I was again on my back sick worse than ever.[95] The Doctors ordered me back to the hospital. Oh! how I hated the idea of returning to those dens of disease and dirt I had so recently left, as I then hoped for ever. It was was my fate and I had but to obey it.

---

nized for ninety days in Confederate service at New Orleans on March 6, 1862. Apparently some of its number chose to go home at the end of their three-month tour of duty, provoking an angry response from Beauregard. In July 1862 it was merged with the 10th Missouri Artillery Battalion. See Napier Bartlett, *Military Record of Louisiana* (Baton Rouge: Louisiana State Univ. Press, 1964), 2:14, 19–20; and Stewart Sefakis, *Compendium of the Confederate Armies: Louisiana* (New York: Facts on File, 1995), 28, 128.

95. The men of the 3d Kentucky dug shallow pits in the ground and drank the water that seeped into them. One of the regiment's historians wrote: "While encamped in and around Corinth the whole command was very seriously afflicted with sickness; hundreds had to be sent away to Lauderdale Springs and other places where hospitals were established for the sick." George, *History of the 3rd, 7th, 8th, and 12th Kentucky*, 33.

There were fifty more of my regiment in the same way as myself, and we were started off from Corinth on the cars, the Drs or any one else not caring a damn where we were sent to or what became of us, so they got [us] off their hands. A box car was all we had for the fifty men and such a night we spent of it no one can describe legs and arms crossed pell mell, and cursing and groaning all night.

The next day we arrived a Vaughan's Station[96] about 5 P.M. Here Dr Blackburn[97] our old Ky Friend, started us all who were able to undertake the journey in a wagon, just as the sun was sitting behind some dark clouds which threatened us with rain before we could get far with our wagon over such ruff roads as led from the station to Yazoo City which place was our destination. The rain soon began to come down in earnest and our backs which were by no means un-used to the like, got as wet as water could make them. We slept however through the most of it so tired and broke down were we and reached Yazoo City a little after day brake—

[*Facing page:* Yazoo City presented a strange look at the time we reached it[. A] great portion of it was flooded by the recent overflow of the river and islands appeared on all sides, trees under water— etc—]

That little town, if I should live a hundred years would always be remembered by me, for the kindness of its citizens, especially of the ladies. Never was I treated with more kindness in my life and this too by strangers. As soon as we arrived the citizens crowded around our wagons to see what they could do for us. Our names were taken and each citizen volunteered to provide for two. Wilson and I fell to the lot of Mr Harrison and Nick Ransdel also all Paducah boys. Charley Ewell and the Fontleroys were taken at one into the coun-try by an old judge and his pretty daughters much to our envy. [*May 20, 1862*] Holt found a relation close by, and all were provided for and but few remained in the temporary hospital after the first day.[98]

96. Vaughan's Station was located on the Mississippi Central Railroad about twenty miles due east of Yazoo City. See George B. Davis et al., *The Official Military Atlas of the Civil War* (New York: The Fairfax Press, 1983), Plate 154.

97. No Dr. Blackburn can be found on the muster rolls of Company D or any of the other companies in the 3d Kentucky.

98. Six soldiers named Wilson and four named Holt served in the 3d Kentucky. Easier to identify on muster rolls were D. W. Ransdall, C. F. Ewell, and R. B. and T. B. Fauntleroy. Kentucky Adjutant General Report, 102. Mr. Harrison was one of the two Harrisons living in Yazoo City: H. Harrison, a merchant, and J. A. Harrison, a

I had not been there but one day and night, before a gentleman living about a mile and a half from town came and got Wilson and myself from the Hospital and took us to his country house. Mr. Richard Powell's[99] kindness will always be remembered with gratitude by me, that is all that a soldier can do. I remained at his house for over a month, at first my health was every day improving, but one day I was out sketching too long in the sun, and in the night I had a congestive chill, as they called it, and it was some time before I got over it. I was sick up to the first of June. Wilson was always by my side indefaticable, often setting up all night with me.

The names of Harrison, Powell, Link, Holt, and Fewques will never be forgotten by the 3d Ky at Yazoo City.[100]

Friday night 30th of May— A grand concert was given for the benefit of the sick Kentucky soldiers. All at the Hospital and in the country were invited, and those who were well enough and could borrow or beg a clean shirt went. The Performance commenced with tableaux and such things as they were would have astonished the world elsewhere. Some of the singing was good. Nick Ransdel was behind the scenes and whistled for the mockingbird in the song listen to the mockingbird—, and was [*June 1862*] called out several times by the audience.

A great commotion took place at Yazoo City— The Yankees were threatening to come up the river in their gunboats and a party of Malitia started to build a raft across the entrance of the river— around which point the gunboats were hovering— We started in grand style with the Malitia on the steamboat "The Dew Drop[101] on the 3d of June— These amateur soldiers, had a great quantity of

---

planter. The "old judge and his pretty daughters" were probably R. S. G. Perkins, an attorney and planter, and his three daughters. Holt's relation was no doubt R. S. Holt, another lawyer and planter. Mississippi, Free Schedules, 8th Census, 1860, vol. 4, Department of the Interior, microfilm reel 131, National Archives, Washington, D.C.

99. There were two Powells living in Yazoo City during the 1860 census, G. M. Powell from Kentucky and J. J. Powell from Virginia, both planters. A thorough search of the records did not turn up a Richard Powell.

100. N. D. Link was a planter of considerable means who had come to Yazoo City from western Canada. "Fewques" could have been L. C. Fuqua.

101. The steamboat *Dew Drop* was built in Cincinnati in 1858 and operated on the Vicksburg-Yazoo River from its home port of Yazoo City before it was burned by the U.S. boats *Forest Rose* and *Linden* on May 25, 1863. The *Dew Drop*'s wreckage

View from the Hospital Door was drawn by Chapman in Yazoo City,
May 23, 1862, while the city was flooded.
Courtesy of the Valentine Museum, Richmond

little nicknacks for the necessities and luxuries of camp life. Muske-
toe bars, cooking utensils of all sizes and shapes, hams, pickles, pre-
serves of all sorts enough to stock a whole brigade of Volunteer
aids and with all this they had but a dozen guns for the party of
thirty. It was fun to hear them boast of what they would do if the
Yanks only showed themselves, and we smiled in our sleaves, and we
four of the third as lookers on enjoyed in the extreme.

When we got to Liverpool[102]—the entrance of the Yazoo we found
these fireside rangers were inclined to do nothing but fish, hunt,
and eat and drink and wanted us to watch out for the Yanks. We
stood the duty for them for a couple of nights and got tired of the
fun and left them the glory of their conceit in imagining that they
were soldiering, and prepared at once to return to our more serious
duties as soldiers in our regiment.

---

at Quiver River, Mississippi, could still be seen in 1959. Frederick Way, Jr., *Way's
Packet Directory, 1848–1983* (Athens: Ohio University Press, 1983), 126.

    102. Liverpool was located on the Yazoo River about nine miles southwest of
Yazoo City; it is not situated "at the entrance of the river." *The Official Military Atlas
of the Civil War*, Plate 154.

On the 15th we left Yazoo City, all the citizens who had been so kind to us were anxious for us to remain longer, but we had already overstaid our time, for we were able to do duty again. A Farewell diner at Mrs. Harrisons and a shake of the hand with our many friends and pearched on wagons, no longer the sick drooping lean invalids, we arrived there but a month before but well and harty and ready for a good long spell of hard service again.

It was on the 19th when we arrived at Tupelo Miss where our regiment had been camped, and found that the whole of Breckenridges Brigade had shifted for parts unknown. We succeeded however in finding out at last the line of march they had taken, which was in the direction of Abbeville. We caught up with them that day. The first member of the Co I overtook was Rosencranz who held up in triumph a letter for me. Who could have written to me, he sang out it is from your home old fellow— I grabbed it and a chocking sensation prevented me from speaking as I recognized my fathers handwriting I hid my emotions as best I could and with trembling hand tore it open, and to hide my emotions, I hunted a shady little neech by the road side and sat down to devour its contense. How happy and thankful I felt after reading it, I had a home still and was

Chapman's watercolor and pencil *Last of June/Camp Magnolia Groves near Vicksburg, 1862*. Courtesy of the Valentine Museum, Richmond.

not forgotten. I was repaid by my fathers forgiving and love for all my suffering, and my mothers few words told me that I had been missed and wished for. So all my many fears to the contrary were dispelled like a troubled dream— That letter opened a new world to me. What could I not endure after that, how different I felt, but a few minutes before I felt like a discarded desolate exile, now I felt as if the whole Confederacy was not large enough for me. I was in a good humour with every one, the world looked brighter to me than it had appeared for many a month. I marched merrily on for the rest of the way to camp a jolly gate.

From Tupelo to Abbeville it was a long tedious march, the dust being so thick that at times you could scarcely see two files ahead, with the scorching June sun beating down on our heads as we tramped along with parched lips, and the hot sandy dust blistering our bare feet. I felt the latter very severly as it was my first experience of marching without shoes. We camped near Abbeville on the 25th and were from the 19th up to this date getting there by the round about way we had to come. We had a few days rest here and on by train to Vicksburg. This was almost the first time they had indulged the Kentucky boys to a ride since we left Bowlingreen and we enjoyed the change very much. We were turned out close to the town and went into camp.

Index

Ten Months in the "Orphan Brigade"

was designed and composed

by Will Underwood

in 10½/14 Monotype Bell

on an Apple G3 using PageMaker

at The Kent State University Press;

printed by sheet-fed offset lithography on

50-pound Turin Book Natural Vellum stock

(an acid-free, totally chlorine-free paper),

Smyth sewn and bound over binder's

boards in Arrestox B cloth,

and wrapped with

dust jackets printed in

3 colors coated with matte film

lamination by Thomson-Shore, Inc.;

and published by

The Kent State University Press

KENT, OHIO 44242